Calvin Milton Woodward

The Educational Value of Manual Training

Consisting of an Examination of the arguments presented in the Report of

the National Council Committee

Calvin Milton Woodward

The Educational Value of Manual Training
*Consisting of an Examination of the arguments presented in the Report of the
National Council Committee*

ISBN/EAN: 9783744692694

Printed in Europe, USA, Canada, Australia, Japan

Cover: Foto ©Suzi / pixelio.de

More available books at **www.hansebooks.com**

THE EDUCATIONAL VALUE

OF

MANUAL TRAINING,

CONSISTING OF AN

EXAMINATION OF THE ARGUMENTS PRESENTED IN THE
REPORT OF THE NATIONAL COUNCIL COMMITTEE ON
PEDAGOGICS, AT NASHVILLE, JULY, 1889,

BY C. M. WOODWARD,

Of Washington University, St. Louis.

AND A CRITICAL REVIEW OF THE SAME REPORT

BY GILBERT B. MORRISON,

Of the Kansas City High School.

WITH AN APPENDIX CONTAINING THE COUNCIL
REPORT IN FULL.

D. C. HEATH & CO., PUBLISHERS,
BOSTON, NEW YORK AND CHICAGO,
1890.

THE EDUCATIONAL VALUE OF MANUAL TRAINING.

There is every indication that the interest in the aims, methods and results of manual training is spreading and deepening. Extravagant notions are being laid aside, and correct and reasonable views are taking their place. Persons who had supposed that there was nothing in it, — that it was only a craze, are finding that there is something in it worthy of consideration and respect. Those wild enthusiasts who claim everything for it are gradually forming a class by themselves quite apart from those who are steadily testing every theory by careful practice.

There is, however, much confusion as to the true scope, meaning and value of manual training. It is my sincere wish to do what I can to give trustworthy information on the subject, to the end that manual training may take its true place in American education. Accordingly, I have gathered here certain reviews and discussions which I hope will be found useful. I do not here present any full discussion of the economic value of manual training, but it must not be inferred that that value is not high. On the contrary, I think its great practical utility would be a sufficient argument for its introduction into certain grades of all schools, were its educational value much less than it is. But its educational value is great as well as its economic, and since I am now concerned in setting forth the former, utility arguments may be left to present themselves. Many people, teachers and others, are prone to consider *direct utility* as unworthy of any place among educational aims.

This leads me to call attention to the universal tendency of public opinion to drive people and institutions into extreme positions. One college officer says that it is no part of the function of an institution that claims to follow a liberal course of study, to give instruction in any *useful* branch. If a branch of science is discovered to have direct practical value, or a line of research is seen to have positive professional worth, that is a sufficient reason for discouraging it. In a similar way it is taken for granted that in a technical school, everything which is not of direct practical value is out of place. There appears to be no institution in which practical and culture studies may be combined. In a recent paper Dr. Harris says: " There remains a permanently valid place for the manual training school for all youths who are old enough to enter a trade and who are unwilling to carry on any further their purely culture studies." — The inference is that if they *are* willing to carry on their purely culture studies, they should not attend a manual training school, no matter how many of such youths there may be nor how long their willingness may continue. — Is it not possible for culture and manual training to go on together? Some persons appear to think that it is not. Classically educated people stare in wide surprise when one happens to speak of Latin and English poetry in the manual training school. With equal surprise they would hear of a Greek student giving a portion of his time to shopwork, or practical electricity. Certain studies admirably suited for both use and discipline are in small favor in

both literary and technical departments of study — in
the former because they are too useful; in the latter
because they are too useless. Now, I claim that both
exclusive and extreme positions are bad; the world
is full of their evil fruits.

This prejudice, which is especially strong in higher
institutions, is plainly seen in the attitude of some educators towards a manual training school. Because a
portion of the curriculum has bearings which are dis-
tinctly practical, useful and economic, it is assumed,
first, that the manual part is purely economic and not
educative; and *secondly*, that all literary and general
education is either omitted from the curriculum or re-
duced to a minimum. I greatly fear that these two
assumptions may be strengthened by the Report on
the "Educational Value of Manual Training," presented to the Council of Education in session at Nashville, Tenn., July 15, 1889. The Report was signed by
Geo. P. Brown (of Illinois), S. S. Parr (now of Minnesota), J. H. Hoose (of N. Y.), and W. T. Harris (now
Commissioner of Education). This Report I propose
to examine somewhat in detail, at least where I disa-
gree. For the sake of immediate reference it is given
in full in the Appendix of this pamphlet.

I suggest to the reader that if he has not already read
the Report, to do so before reading my criticisms. He
will observe that in the outset, the Committee "have
proposed in their report to inquire in what precisely
consists the educative value of the branches taught in
the manual training school." ˙ Yet in spite of this laud-
able purpose the reader will find that the instruction
given in a manual training school receives but scant attention in the Report. He will find a large number of

subjects discussed, which have no connection, or only a
remote one, with the nature and purpose of manual
training.   There are homilies on Street Gamins, Arrested Development, Conduct, Illiteracy, and The Study
of Pure Science, as though these were pertinent to their
declared purpose.   What I regard as misleading and
erroneous in the Report is these fugitive side-discussions
and incidental definitions.   It is not so much what the
Committee actually declare, with one or two exceptions,
as what they lead the reader to infer, that is most ob-
jectionable, as I shall soon proceed to show.

The Report has already been published five or six
times, and no doubt has been widely read.   I ask from
friends and foes alike a candid consideration both of
the Report and of the criticisms which are submitted
herewith.   It seems to me that one coming to the Report for information, with no previous clear notion of
manual training, its purpose and its scope, must get
from its perusal a widely erroneous conception of the
nature and mission of the educational feature known as
manual training.

I have no idea that there was any intention to mis-
lead on the part of the writer of the Report, but that it
is misleading I feel quite sure.   Evidently the Committee had in mind the "uncompromising enemies" of
public education fully as much as "the advocates of
manual training."   In the very first paragraph the Report declares that those two classes are united.   I think
that a grave mistake.   Manual training people have no
fellowship with the enemies of public schools.

Under the cover of an attack upon manual training
the Committee deals its heaviest blows upon those "uncompromising enemies" who oppose all literary educa-

tion at the public expense. None of such blows actually hit us, but the unwary are liable to think that they do and that we deserve them. They naturally ask: "Unless the enemies and the manual people are under the same flag, why this attack on the opponents of spiritual education under the cover of the Educational Value of Manual Training?"

Now the people who are engaged in carrying on manual training schools are to a man heartily in favor of public schools; most of them are public school people, and they all believe in the value and necessity of literary and scientific training. But they believe in more than that, — they believe in incorporating manual training in the higher grades, and they most firmly maintain that public education will thereby be improved.

I shall take up several points in the Report in a certain logical order.

I.

THE CURRICULUM OF THE MANUAL TRAINING SCHOOL.

The Council Report says that "the entire curriculum of the manual training school," is included in " work in the trades that deal in wood and metals."

How can the Committee justify the use of such language? The vast majority of teachers and parents have never seen a manual training school; have had no chance to know what one is and how it is conducted. These people naturally look with confidence to the deliberate utterance of a committee of the Council, the most august body of Educators in the land. One of the important questions of the hour is: What is the real value of a manual training school? Prelim-

inary to this is the question : What *is* a manual training
school? And this distinguished Committee says that
the "ENTIRE curriculum of the manual training school
is included in work in the trades!"

It is not easy to account for such a careless statement. It seems probable that having fixed their minds
upon shop-exercises, they, for the moment, laid aside
all thought of anything else. I shall recur to this point
at a later stage of this discussion, but I cannot refrain
from remarking that in this respect their report seriously misrepresents manual training schools. Let us
call it a slip of the pen ; they wrote " entire curriculum," instead of " the entire tool-work of the curriculum." But we do not expect such men to slip in that
way.

Now what are the " cold " facts in regard to the curriculum of the manual training schools? I think I can
answer for nearly every one of them : —

First. The curriculum gives one-half as much time to
drawing as to tool-work.

Second. It gives as much time (study and recitation)
to mathematics as to tool-work.

Third. It gives as much time to Science (theoretical
and practical) as to tool-work.

Fourth. It gives as much time to language and literature as to tool-work.

No "trades" teach drawing, or mathematics, or
science, or literature. All these things must be included to make up the curriculum *entire* of a manual
training school. In confirmation, see the catalogues of
the manual training schools of Chicago, Baltimore,
Philadelphia, Toledo, San Francisco, St. Paul, Cambridge and St. Louis.

In the face of these truths, how unfortunate the Committee's statement is! And as I reread the entire report, I see that it was no slip of pen. In numerous passages the reader sees the same statement assumed. I quote from the report : —

"Your Committee understand that any amount of manual training conducted in a school is no equivalent for the school education in letters and science, *and ought not to be substituted for it.*
"The economic utilitarian opposition to the spiritual education in our schools, makes sure of his [the pupil's] inability to ascend above manual toil *by cutting off his purely intellectual training.*
"The *illiterate manual laborer*, no matter how skillfully educated for his trade in wood and metal operations, cannot read and write.
"To be excellent in manual training, would not prevent him [the pupil] from being *illiterate* and a bad neighbor and a bad citizen,— *even a dynamiter.*" [The Italics are mine.]

They speak of the manual training school as a "school devoted to the business of educating the youth in the essentials of his trade or vocation."

There are other passages of similar import which the reader may readily find in the Report for himself. Now what idea of a manual training school is a parent or teacher to get from such passages as those? We are bound to suppose there is some relevancy in them, yet if they are not as misleading as language can be, I do not understand my mother-tongue.

But the Committee may have knowledge which has been denied to me. They may have found in Illinois, or Indiana, or Massachusetts, a manual training school either in existence or in prospect which has "cut out

letters and science and all purely intellectual training;"
where the boys are "illiterate, unable to read and
write;" where the managers of the school are making
sure of the boys' "inability to rise above manual toil"
by "making their childhood a preparation for special
industries," with a strong probability that they will become bad neighbors, bad citizens, and even dynamiters.

If they have found such a school,* their language has
some justification, and I heartily join them in condemn-
ing it, root and branch. Let all who believe as I do in
the value of cultured minds, as well as skillful hands,
join in frowning such a school out of real or possible
existence, and do what they can to establish the general adoption of a rational curriculum. Meanwhile let
the Committee amend their report; give credit where
credit is due, and avoid the danger of being suspected
of setting up a "straw-man" for the exquisite pleasure
of seeing it topple over under their vigorous blows.

Unless the Committee can justify their words by reference to some such obnoxious manual training school,

---

* In answer to this charge of misrepresentation, Supt. Parr
has replied: —

"Truth is not geographical in its boundaries. Fortunately it
is not to be viewed as circumscribed by the corporation lines of
great cities, like Philadelphia, Chicago and St. Louis, whose manual training schools are cited as a larger truth against the smaller
truth from country districts like Illinois, Indiana and Minnesota."

This suggests that he has found in the country districts of
those three States manual training schools of the very objection-
able sort. I am sorry that such schools exist, but I am very glad
that Mr. Parr has found them. Let us all hope that they may
mend their ways. But Supt. Parr should be careful how he speaks
of "country districts." I gave great offense once by referring to
one of our most accomplished educational writers as a "country
editor in Illinois."

we shall conclude that not a phrase only, but the greater part of their report was a slip, and should have been submitted under another title.

When the above criticism was made in the pages of THE TEACHER, the chairman of the Committee, Mr. Geo. P. Brown, was constrained to reply. He ridiculed the idea that any one could be misled by their statement in regard to the curriculum. Of course, every one knew that manual training schools had more or less work in science and literature, but the educational value of such work was not under discussion. What was wanted was a definite statement and analysis of the educational value of manual training. Said he : "The Report was upon the educational value of manual training *considered by itself, disconnected from the study of letters and science,* and *without any regard to where it was obtained,* and the St. Louis school or *the education received in it was not in the minds of the Committee* while making it."

This is a most astonishing confession. Mr. Brown admits that although they claimed to inquire into the "educative value of the branches taught in the manual training school," yet in writing their report no thought of the education received in the manual training school entered their minds. They did not even go into the schools to see what their tool-work was and how it was taught. On the contrary, they went outside, among manual laborers, where labor (not "training") was not complicated by a knowledge and study of science and letters. Taking Mr. Brown's confession and the Report together we see where they went. They went among the street gamins, and noted their stunted pre-maturity. They went into the factories which employ child labor, and almost wept over the deformed bodies and joyless lives of the helpless victims they found. They went among the illiterate craftsmen and enumerated the great number of things they ought to know, but of which they knew nothing. They went among the rioters of a great city, all of whom were " excellent in manual training," but wanting in all the characteristics of good citizens and good neighbors.

Then they returned from their inquiry and prepared their Report. Now, unless they have stultified themselves, they wish their millions of readers to understand that the evils they have witnessed — the arrested development, the deformity, the wretchedness, the ignorance, and the crime, — are to be taken as indicative of the educative value of manual training as taught in the manual training school. If they are not to be taken to mean that, then what in the name of reason are they to be taken for ?

Hands without brains are as worthless as brains without hands. Mr. Brown has been satisfied with the latter; I suppose it in accordance with the law of extremes for him to expect us to be satisfied with the former. It is now evident that he believes that the processes and activities of manual training as taught in school, and closely associated at every step with science and letters, are identical with the mental and physical processes and activities of uneducated laborers, toiling for daily bread in commercial establishments.

This defense of Mr. Brown, that in order to observe the effect of manual training pure and simple, it is necessary to go among people whose *only* training is in the manual direction, has little in its favor. In the first place, there are no people whose moral, physical and intellectual status may be attributed to manual training and to nothing else. Secondly, the sort of training that people get in practical work outside of schools cannot be compared in educative effect with the systematic and logical work given in tool-work and drawing in a manual training school. Thirdly, to find the educative value of a feature of school training, it must be considered as it is given in connection with other school work. It is utterly unreasonable and unfair to take it out of its environment. We do not test values thus in other matters. In estimating the value of salt as an ingredient of our food, it is not necessary to hunt up a people who eat nothing but salt, and observe its effects upon them. In determining the educative value of the study of Italian, it is not necessary to analyze the character and condition of a swarthy native of Venice or Naples, selling fruit and peanuts at the corner, or vending plaster images from door to door. To be sure, his education is limited to an unscientific knowledge of his native tongue, and may be held to be free from all other branches of culture, and we may pay no " regard to where it was obtained."

I insist that the influence of manual training in school education shall be. studied under the conditions in which it is given in education. There is absolutely no question about its educative value under other conditions. We are discussing schools and school-work, and nothing else. If the influence of manual training *as it is taught in manual training schools* and in connection with all the other school work is not yet sufficiently manifest in the lives and characters of those who have received it, then let us not attempt to give it by reasoning from effect to cause. Leave that phase of the discussion till adequate data are at hand, and confine the present discussion to an analysis of the character and content of manual training, and, reasoning from cause to effect, determine its influence upon the minds and characters of school boys.

It may be answered that the Report gives such an analysis and such a course of reasoning. Such a claim I should flatly deny, for the processes it analyzes are those of factories and not of schools, and then, for the most part, it attempts to determine the influence of such factory methods on illiterate, unscientific people. But the difference between school work and factory work needs to be set forth at length.

II.

SCHOOL TOOL-WORK VS. TRADE-WORK.

Assuming that the Council Committee meant the " entire tool-work of the curriculum," let us compare it with trade-work. Let us see if it is all " included in trades that deal in wood and metals," as the Report would have us believe.

It is true that all our actual tool-work is included in trade operations, just as all arithmetic is included in the business of the grocer, the jeweler, the druggist, the banker, the plasterer, etc. ; and as all natural science is included in the work of engineers and manufacturers. Those are strong points in favor of tool-work, arithmetic and science. If there were no use, no applications of arithmetic in life, it would be as little taught as is Chinese.

But the converse statements are by no means true.

No trade is included in our tool-work, just as no occupation is included in science and mathematics. Let me dwell a moment upon the striking difference between our work and ordinary trade-work.

The false statement most easily made and most often heard is that the manual training school aims to turn out carpenters and blacksmiths; and the Report encourages that notion by admitting "in the outset, the reasonableness of substituting a system of manual training in special schools for the old system of apprenticeship."

Suppose a man learns the trade of a carpenter, what does he learn to do? He learns to lay a floor, to make a panel-door, to build a cornice, to shingle a roof, to construct a picket-fence, to build a flight of stairs, to put in headers in floor joists, to frame a barn, and to cut rafters for a hip-roof. Unless he can do all or most of these things, he is no carpenter. Our students, as a rule, never do any of these things. The joinery, wood-carving, wood-turning, and pattern-making we give our students have small reference to particular trades, though as the exercises deal with the theory of tools and with the elements of construction, they may be said to underlie a score of trades.

But the fact that at every stage of our work drawing is interwoven with the use of tools, and the fact that attention is always called to what is general and what is special in the exercise, make our wood-work a different thing from the work of any industrial establishment.

Similarly a worker at the forge and anvil can scarcely be called a blacksmith till he has skillfully made and set a horseshoe, welded and fitted the tire of a wagon wheel, forged and sharpened heavy drills, and made a certain number of bolts or nails in an hour.

We aim to do none of these things, so that gauged by such a standard our students are acquiring something very different from blacksmithing. They fairly learn the *principles* of metal forging, and they have had just practice enough to enable them to thoroughly understand and appreciate those principles. They know, for instance, that when the thread-end of a tie-rod has been enlarged by up-setting, the rod is stronger than when a larger end has been welded on instead; and they know *why* it is stronger, and their knowledge has a quality about it which is altogether lacking in the knowledge one gains from reading such a statement in a book.

But some one will ask, is not this knowledge of principles, and this personal experience valuable to one who does subsequently learn the full details of a metal trade? Of course it is, immensely valuable; in fact, I do not see how any really intelligent and successful worker can get on without it; nor can I conceive of any reasonably active mode of life, in which this knowledge and experience would not be of great value as a species of practical science culture.

The second error then to which I would call attention is that of regarding the shop-work, which is appropriate for a school, as adequate for apprenticeship. If at the age of 17, 18, or 19, the manual graduate desires to learn a trade, he must still serve a brief apprenticeship in a strictly trade establishment where not principles but definite practices are taught. But this he can do with numerous and important advantages on his side. His knowledge of drawing, of science, of mathematics, of letters and of the fundamental principles and processes of construction fit him for speedy leadership among the old style, uneducated mechanics.

III.

THE AGE OF MANUAL TRAINING SCHOOL PUPILS.

In the very beginning of their Report, the Committee propose " to inquire in what precisely consists the educative value of the branches taught in the manual training school." They say that they will "treat incidentally also the economic questions involved."

After assuming that the " branches taught" consist exclusively of trade work, and conceding their superiority to the old style of apprenticeship, they " insist that *such manual training* ought not to be begun before the completion of the twelfth year of the pupil."

Incredible as it may appear, the Committee *insist*, as though in the face of some determined opposition, that boys shall not devote their time exclusively to learning trades *before they are twelve years old!* For the sake of emphasis they repeat :

" They hold the opinion that neither apprenticeship nor the industrial school should be allowed to take possession of the youth until the completion of his twelfth year at least; the fifteenth year is still better, because physical maturity is necessary for the formation of the best muscular movements to produce skill. At too early an age the pupil with his small hands and fingers, his short and undeveloped arms, is obliged to acquire bad habits of holding the implements of labor. Moreover, the serious occupations of life cannot be imposed on children without dwarfing their human nature —

physically, intellectually and morally — and producing arrested development. Not only the games of youth, but the youth's freedom from the cares of mature life should be insured to him if the best preparation is to be made for manhood."

The Report then dwells on the sad spectacle presented by the unschooled children of the very poor, the street gamin, and the premature old age of those whose childhood has been usurped by suffering and care.

As I said in reference to former quotations, we are bound to suppose that all this has something to do with manual training and the manual training school.

The Committee does not say outright that manual training schools are attempting to teach trades to children not twelve years old, but they plainly give one to understand that they do, and that these dreadful evils are likely to follow as their legitimate fruit. Unless these evils exist or are imminent in our manual training schools; unless those schools do cramp the small hands and fingers, the short and undeveloped arms of tender children, dwarfing and stunting both body and mind by hard labor, premature care, and cheerless drudgery, — why does the Committee interpolate the sad picture? Did they consciously or unconsciously hope or expect that, because we all condemn cruelty and injustice to children, we should be led by this juxtaposition in their report to condemn manual training schools also?

I suspect that my readers, who have seen the Report, and who have gotten from it some notions of the institution, whose educative and economic value the Committee set out to investigate, will suffer no small surprise when told that not only is there no physical, intellectual and moral dwarfing in the manual training school, no imposition of the serious occupations of life, no lack of joy and cheer, but that *no manual training school* that I know of *admits pupils till they are thirteen or fourteen years old.*

The usual age corresponds to the *ninth year in school;* in some cases it is the eighth year or possibly the seventh, *provided* the boy be thirteen years old. The average age of the 100 boys who form the " first-year class " of the St. Louis Manual Training School, and who were admitted on the 16th of September, 1889, was 15 years, 11 months. The youngest boy in the class was 13 years, 8 months old. In the manual training schools of Chicago, Philadelphia, Cleveland, New York, Cambridge, Indianapolis, Albany, Minneapolis, and San Francisco, the age is about the same as in my school. In those of Baltimore, Toledo, Omaha, Springfield, Mass., New Orleans, and St. Paul, the age may be a little less.

Manual training schools are springing up so rapidly (that is, public high schools are becoming manual training schools in so many cities and large towns), that I cannot speak definitely of many of them. The Commissioner appointed by the Governor of Pennsylvania to investigate the subject of manual training as related to public education, reported in favor of the introduction of manual training (shop-work and drafting) into *all the high schools in the State.*

I do not ignore the fact that the country is full of insane people, and that not a few indulge in educational vagaries. Perhaps the Pedagogical Committee have come in contact with some of them, and have mistaken

them for manual training school people.   But I "insist"
that in discussing the value of the manual training school,
they shall take the school *as it is,* and not as some irre-
sponsible party — I was about to say "crank" — may
imagine it to be.   [It will be observed that I am not
speaking of *my* manual training school, but of *the*
manual training school.]

I have met some of these mad people.   They always
find much fault with us.   They think we might do and
ought to do numerous things that I know very well we
cannot do, and would be very foolish to try to do.
These erratic people generally are unfamiliar with scientific methods of teaching, and as ignorant of what
trades really are and the conditions under which they
may be adequately mastered as I am of oil painting.

It may be objected that the Committee were dealing
with the question of manual training in all the grades as
it has been introduced in some cities and as it has been
urged by excellent people for all cities.   Of course I
cannot know all that has been done in the name of
manual training, but so far as my acquaintance does ex-
tend, the manual training work which has been tried
in the lower grades [of New Haven, or Montclair, or
New York City, for instance,] is as far as possible from
"trade work in woods and metals."   The exercises
consist only of paper-cutting, drawing, clay-modeling,
whittling, and a few simple exercises in joinery with the
older classes.   There may be a little turning, scroll-
sawing and filing, but it is too little to justify any of the
assumptions of our Committee.   So far as I know the
views of teachers who have had actual experience with
regular tool instruction, I am able to say that they are
almost unanimously opposed to giving shop-work to

boys less than thirteen years of age. Editor Brown has repeatedly called me an advocate of manual training as an "integral part of the curriculum of the common schools." I am not quite sure that I know what he means by "integral," but from the context I infer that he means that I advocate the introduction of regular shop-work in all the grades, primary, intermediate and high. But I advocate no such thing, and I do not think I have ever written or said a word which can fairly be interpreted as conveying any such notion.

In conclusion, I challenge the Committee to point out a single school in the United States, manual training or otherwise, where pupils not 12 years of age are set to learning trades. If they cannot do so, it will be in order for them to explain why they devote so much time and space to an essay on "street gamins," "child labor," and physical deformity, and to insisting that we shall not do what no one has ever done, and what no sane man wishes to do.

IV.

SOCIAL EVILS AS RELATED TO MANUAL TRAINING.

In continuing my criticism, I wish to say that there are many things in the Report which I should heartily approve were they removed from all connection with the discussion of manual training, Take, for instance, a long passage in which the Committee answers the question: "What does one need to know besides his trade?" They answer correctly and well under these heads: Behavior towards Fellow-Workmen, Employers, Neighbors, Family, Children, Fellow-Citizens,

Votes, Voters ; Evils of Illiteracy ; Victims of Agita-
tors ; Geography, History, Literature.

Why, of course ! It goes without saying that there
is no difference of opinion among respectable people
on these points. But in what way does such a discussion bear upon the educative value or economy of
manual training ?

Could they not with equal force and propriety
discuss the needs of personal cleanliness, the care of
the teeth, diet, the use of tobacco, whisky, etc. ?

I suppose the Committee will reply, at least in
thought, that these matters are not in any peculiar manner related to manual labor, while the evils they point
out are characteristic of laborers and craftsmen.

Possibly they are — but still I ask, why was the point
introduced? Had the Report been written to set forth
the educative value of the study of the Greek language,
this disquisition on Social Evils would have been just as
appropriate as now. The passage referred to appears
to be introduced to point out " a fatal omission on the
part of the economist," who claims that " the schools
should fit the child for his future duties in life."

We are not told who the " economist " is, nor is it
shown that in truth he makes the " fatal omission," but
we have here a clew to the Committee's reason for pre-
senting their homily on Conduct : *First*, they assume
that the economist is asking for the manual training
school; and *secondly*, they assume that the manual
training school is an institution to multiply laborers and
craftsmen of the sort who know nothing besides their
trades. In other words, they have gone into the pin-
factories, plow-factories and forge-factories, the street
mobs, and into the jails of Chicago, and they have said :

" These pin-makers, these plow-handle turners,* these blacksmiths, these illiterate bad neighbors, and these dynamiters are manual laborers, and they typify the legitimate fruit of manual training and of an attempt to fit boys for their future duties in life !"

The magnitude of the Committee's error in all this is past measuring. Those unfortunate men exhibit the fruit not of manual-training-school education, but of a want of it. If they are the fruit of anything, they are the fruit of that system of education which has prevailed ever since they were born, and which our Committee would fain have us be contented with as adequate to all communities and to all times. Instead of trying to bolster up their attack upon manual training by an enumeration of the shortcomings of those ill-trained people who unquestionably make up the mass of laborers

---

* A word of explanation is necessary here. Mr. Brown is the editor of a school journal, and he has naturally discussed manual training in its pages. Once he wrote : —

"A man in one of the manufacturing towns of this State has been turning plow-handles for twenty years. Day after day his life has been one monotonous round of toil. Ten hours per day for twenty years has matured the turning of plow-handles into a mental and physical habit which dominates and even constitutes his life. When two-thirds to three-fourths of the curriculum of lower grades, and one-half of the higher is devoted to work akin to turning plow-handles, is it not a serious question whether it gives the preparation which that man most needs that is to turn plow-handles all his life ? "

If I believed, as of course Mr. Brown does, that the friends of manual training were laboring to bring about the condition of things pictured in the above quotation, I should oppose manual training so vigorously that I should put Mr. Brown's opposition to the blush. " *Two-thirds to three-fourths of the curriculum of the lower grades!!* " Great Scott! " *Devoted to work akin to turning plow-handles!!* " Shade of Horace! Can the man be mad ?

in this country to-day, they should see that had manual
training schools been as numerous during the past thirty
years as have high schools and academies, the evils
they complain of would be much less than they now
are.

This for two reasons : (1) The number of boys carrying their education forward into their teens would
have been vastly greater than it has been without such
schools; and (2) though not teaching special crafts,
but general principles; giving a wide range of culture
instead of aiming to put boys into trades and professions, — had the number of manual training schools
been adequate to the wants of the community, three
striking results would have followed : —

(*a*) There would have been a greater industrial development, particularly along new lines and into new
fields, though the relative number of craftsmen would
scarcely have been increased.

(*b*) The amount, variety, and quality of industrial
products would have been greatly increased and improved.

(*c*) The average tone and character of our home-
trained industrial workers would have been substantially
raised above its present level; they would have been
much better educated than they now are, for manual
training means not *less* but *more* education.

This analysis does not include the benefit that would
have accrued to other occupations, not industrial, from
the wholesome training of the same schools.

Though the Committee set out to discover "the educative value of the branches taught in the manual training school," they have done no such thing; they have
only taken up the question: What is the educative value

of *ordinary manual labor with tools*, as practiced by those who have had *no other education of any sort;* who know neither how to behave, how to read, how to draw, nor how to vote?

I therefore convict the Committee of a piece of most illogical reasoning, to wit: They condemn manual training schools on account of evils for which they are in no way responsible, but which, on the contrary, it is a part of their high mission to help remove.

V.

MANUAL TRAINING COMPARED WITH THE STUDY OF PURE SCIENCE.

The Report begins the discussion of the educative phase of manual training with an admirable statement : —

"The education of the intellect takes place through the ascent from one thought or idea to another; from a narrow point of view to a broader and more comprehensive one; from a vague and general grasp of a subject to an insight that explains all the details, and sees the relations of all parts to the whole."

I ask for nothing better than that on which to base criticisms. Equally good is another which I shall also be glad to use at another time. I insert it here because the two come side by side in the report, and both are worthy of high praise : —

"The education of the will takes place by fixing and unfixing habits of doing."

The report presents an argument based on science to

prove that the intellectual education gained from
manual training is of narrow scope and limited in time.
The argument is of the *a fortiori* sort.

(*a*) "The study of pure science is more educative
intellectually than the study of special applications of
it."

(*b*) "The study of applications of science is more
educative than the labor of making the machine."

Therefore, *a fortiori*, the study of pure science is much
more educative intellectually than the labor of making
the machine.   This conclusion is not formally stated,
but of course it is easily inferred.   In proof of the first
point (*a*), the Report compares the study of the steam
engine with "the study of the theory of heat and of
the dynamics of elastic fluids."   The second point, (*b*),
rests upon the consideration that the maker of a
machine adopts one design out of many, one material
out of several, and "obscures his general view of the
principle of the machine by covering it up with a great
collection of details that do not essentially concern it."

The Report leaves the reader to make the application
of this argument for himself.   Of course it is to be
understood that the manual training pupil is the maker
of "the machine."   It is not very clear what "the
machine" is, but perhaps the steam engine is meant.
It would also appear to be understood that the machine-
maker does not study the applications of science
beyond the limits of his particular machine, and that he
gives no attention whatever to the general theory of
heat and the dynamics of elastic fluids.   Moreover, it
would appear that the educational object of making the
machine can only be to acquire thereby some view of
the principle of the machine.   The conclusion of the

argument was explicitly stated by Mr. Harris, the writer of the Report, in closing the debate upon it. He said:

"The purely manual work of the school belongs to the lowest grade, and furnishes the obscurest knowledge of principles covered up by a mass of non-essential circumstances."

There are many things to be said in answer to this argument. First, I will meet the Committee on their own ground, that of the study of science. In the second place, I will show that their ground is not our ground, and that in this case, as in many others, they have not yet divined the motive nor the content of tool-work.

1. The study of pure science, the theories of heat, pneumatics, hydraulics, electricity, chemical affinity, etc., are not omitted in a manual training school. Of course, the students are young and capable of only elementary work.

Moreover, the study of pure science is coupled with a large variety of special applications. Instead of debating the question which is best, pure science without applications, or applications without pure science, we have *both*, with a perfect assurance that the two combined are greatly superior to either alone. In the next place, our students make a great variety of apparatus to illustrate special applications of scientific principles. For instance, they actually make pumps, fountains, pyrometers, telephones, dynamos, engines, telegraphic apparatus, cameras, etc., etc. [Of course the more elaborate of these things are made as "projects" by individual students at the very end of their course.] And we find that their work with minute and exact details in real wood, iron, steel, brass, copper, leather, tin and glass, *does not obscure* their general view of the principles of science, but that it makes it wonderfully clear. Their minds "ascend from one thought to another, from a narrow point of view to a broader and more comprehensive one: from a vague and general grasp to a clear insight." The narrow point of view must come before the broad one. The best possible beginning is to thoroughly master certain experimental phenomena, and the best way to know an experiment is to know the apparatus root and branch.*

Did Tyndall or Faraday obscure his view of science by manufacturing his own apparatus? Did Edison obscure his view of the theory of electricity by manufacturing his hundreds of devices with his own hands? Does the musician obscure his general view of the principles of music by the thorough mastery of a particular exercise or piece? Can any one have a *comprehensive* view of the whole unless he has a clear and comprehensive view of the parts?

Mr. Harris himself once said most happily, while comparing the primitive knowledge which one gets for

---

* Speaking of the apparatus used to illustrate the principles of science in school laboratories, Prof. John F. Woodhull says: "Most pupils of high-school age fail to comprehend the machines, and their minds are only confused thereby with reference to the principles."

"As discussions about words can never remove the difficulties that exist in things, so no skill in the use of those aids to thought which language furnishes can relieve us from the necessity of a *prior and more direct study of the things* which are the subjects of our reasonings. And *the more exact and the more complete that study of things has been*, the more likely shall we be to employ with advantage all symbolic aids and appliances." — *Preface to "Boole's Differential Equations."*

himself with mere second-hand hearsay knowledge :
" A very little primary knowledge is worth more than
a cargo of secondary knowledge." All primary knowledge begins with details.

On the other hand, what confidence can one have in
a mere theorizer? one who knows nothing of special
applications? And if he has studied applications
under ideal conditions only, where machines are purely
imaginary, with imponderable, inextensible, invincible,
and perfectly rigid or perfectly flexible material ; if he
knows by experience nothing of the details of apparatus made of real materials and used under actual conditions, — is he not lacking in many essential elements
of a sound scientific training ?

In my judgment the field of pure science lies far
beyond the range of the manual training school, in
the higher realms of the technical school. The pupil
must creep before he can walk, and he must walk before he can run. In the manual training school we can
hardly claim to do more than to help him to walk.
His point of view is narrow, his horizon near, but if he
sees clearly what he sees at all, and grasps firmly what
he puts his hand to, he will with increasing strength
and a broader vision "ascend from thought to thought,"
to a just conception of the scope and meaning of
science.

My answer is, then, that, on the assumption that the
exercises of the shop of the manual training school
consist solely of machine-making, for the purpose of
illustrating the principles and applications of pure
science, their argument still does not touch us, for our
plan of *combining theory and practice* is a vast improve-
ment over either alone.

2. The chief purpose of our shop-work is *not the study of science* as that phrase is ordinarily understood. The work I referred to above, that of constructing and using physical and chemical apparatus, is quite distinct from our regular course of shop-work. Of course, there is more or less science in all shop-work, for every mechanical process and the form and theory of every tool are based on established principles of science; yet the main object of shop exercise is not to gain a knowledge of those established principles.

Just here is the stumbling block of many an inquirer. It is often assumed that we must have one or more of these three objects in maintaining tool-work in school, viz.:

1. To produce articles for the market or for domestic use.

2. To teach specific trades to those who wish or expect to follow them.

3. To teach and illustrate the principles of practical science.

Let me give the Committee credit for not holding the first opinion. I am not so sure as to their standing on the second point. As to the third point, the argument I quoted above appears to show that the Pedagogical Committee regard our tool-work as only a poor, narrow method of·studying science.

None of the three objects are ours.

The primary object of tool-work (for there are many secondary objects) is *to develop and strengthen productive activity by gaining a mastery over materials and certain conventional tools and processes.* ·What we shall do with our materials and tools after we have mastered them we do not particularly inquire. They are suited to abundant uses, and the active mind will need them a thousand times in embodying thought and in effecting other ends. The most efficient method of arousing and stimulating the executive faculties is by giving one the sense of mastership over materials, forces, and appliances. One quickly desires to do what he first sees he has the power to do. The sense of mastership, of ability to smash, to break, to overthrow, which leads the undisciplined, unskilled youth, to commit vandalism, may be converted into a sense of ability to build, to invent, to construct, to create ; which leads to such things, as book-cases, dynamos, engines and cameras.

This conversion cannot be effected without teaching minutely what book-cases, dynamos, engines, and cameras are ; and secondly, giving a mastery of the materials and tools to be used, and the principles of construction.

But while gaining this mastery, ulterior objects are kept out of sight, just as we keep the sonatas of Beethoven and the nocturnes of Chopin out of the sight of a child absorbed in the intricacies of scales, fingering, and counting exercises on the piano.

For example (and I think it best to be quite minute on this point, for here is where many fail to appreciate our methods), we teach the boy how to grind his plane and oil-stone it, till it has a razor edge without flaw or feather. Then we teach him by precept and by example how to set his plane; to take it to pieces; to readjust it to the nature of his material ; how to hold and push it so as to avoid unequal cutting on a side or at the end of a piece, — and all this without any particular thought as to what he will make with his plane when he has mastered it.

In a similar way he is taught the proper care and use of every tool on his list. He learns how to work with, against, across, and on the end of the grain, with all kinds of wood from Apple and Ash to Walnut and Willow. He learns how to treat a knot; how to use the brace and bits; how to avoid splitting when nailing, chiseling and boring; how to use try-square, gauge, and bevel, in accurately laying out mortices, dove-tails, etc.; how to hold his chisel and how to strike with the mallet; how to saw to a fit on the right or left of a line; how to match and glue, and polish, etc.

The pupil learns all these things abstracted from special applications. No lively interest in some proposed construction is allowed to " obscure his view " of the details of the work which must be mastered one by one. While making a joint, for instance, nothing is allowed to interfere with a full comprehension of its nature, its exact form and dimensions, and the order in which the steps of the process may best be executed· The question of what is to be done with the joint is not allowed to come in till he has thoroughly learned not only to draw it, but to make it.

In these several respects we teach tool-work and the properties of materials just as we do the details of algebra. Addition, subtraction, factoring, equations, elimination, and so forth, are taught without much reference to the uses of algebra in the study of physics, mechanics, astronomy and the higher mathematics. As a rule the teachers of algebra have no conception of its use beyond the solution of problems '' made up '' as illustrations. The real problems which gave rise to algebra, not one teacher in a thousand knows anything about.

Moreover, we give our student workmen facts to reason upon before we set them to formal reasoning.
Scientific theories are the product of mature and well-
informed minds. There is in recent educational efforts
to teach the principles of science, far too much of a cer
tain sort of shallow generalizing on one or two facts,
and these more often borrowed or supposed than observed.

Hence, while teaching the use of the chisel and plane
and knife, we say scarce a word about the theory of the
wedge, and the inclined plane; while giving instruction
in the use of the mallet, hammer and sledge, we say
little about momentum and kinetic energy; while
teaching the exact and delicate operations of cutting
V-threaded and square-threaded bolts and nuts we
barely refer to the theory of the screw and to co-effi-
cients of friction. By the time our pupils get far
enough in our analytic method of shop-work, to be able
to make an entire steam engine, they are near the end
of the course and are familiar with an elementary theory
of such engines. Having gained a fair mastery over
materials and tools, they are now able to use them in
the study of general principles and in the expression of
thought.

If this mastery is well gained they have conquered a
new world, a world full of thought and valuable experience, a department of knowledge fraught with wide
uses and a generous human interest. With it one can
never fail to be stronger, clearer, surer in dealing with
the problems and duties of real life. In spite of the
high authority of the Committee, the mastership of
materials, tools, and industrial processes is educative in
a high degree. The kind of knowledge acquired is far

reaching in its applications and far more invigorating
to the mind than the masses of details and circumstances that surround certain literary studies * which
painfully impress many people competent to judge, as
unhappily neither educative nor essential to any rational
theory. Mr. Harris once said that a child trained for
one year in a kindergarten would acquire a skillful use
of his hands and a habit of accurate measurement of
the eye which would be his possession for life. How
can I adequately express the value of the rich and varied
possessions gained by a boy in his teens, having a daily ·
exercise of from one to two hours for three or four
school-years in a good series of school-shops!

From this brief and imperfect sketch (for I have
touched only upon a very few of the details of the manual branches taught in every good manual training
school) it must be seen that there is no occasion for
making comparisons, disparaging or otherwise, between
the study of science pure or applied, and manual training. The two must go on side by side, and instead of
trying to belittle one at the expense of the other we
should aim to perfect both. This latter aim we greatly
help by combining the two. No science-teaching without shop-work can possibly be as efficient as it easily
becomes with it; and again, no shop-work carried on
in a school where no science is taught can possibly be as
luminous with thought, as where the two are carefully
taught side by side. They are strong allies, and inci-
dentally they serve each other continually.

Thus do I answer the argument of the report based

---

* Such as " memorizing the etymological trash from the lumber
room of antiquity." — *Report of Supt. Wm. T. Harris.*

on a comparison of the study of science with an assumed unscientific construction of individual machines; and thus do I show that while the Committee reasons badly on its own ground, its ground is not at all our ground, and that their argument is entirely irrelevant.

Dr. Harris, in his Ohio paper on the relation of high schools to colleges, says that while a knowledge of natural science, modern literature, and universal history was not demanded nor expected from an educated man one hundred years ago, things are now so changed that no man can pass for educated without more or less minute acquaintance with them. They have become recognized as " conventionalities of intelligence."

To that statement, which I accept, I would add that a more or less complete mastery of the materials, tools, and processes which underlie the vast industrial developments of this age of scientific applications is fast becoming one of the " conventionalities of intelligence." It will no longer satisfy nor suffice to claim that a knowledge of the details of good workmanship, of the practical arts which underlie manual skill in whatever field of industry, has neither dignity nor educational worth. No Council Committee can be allowed to dispose of it as "a mass of non-essential circumstances."

There is danger that some unconventional fellow will voice public sentiment by some word meaning "over-conservative " while speaking of the Committee and their Report.

Mr. Brown in particular is very sensitive to the term "old fogy," which possibly some one has been rude enough to apply to him. I should be sorry to believe that he deserves the title; but let him not flatter himself that the list of "conventionalities of intelligence"

4

has been closed. If he is left behind as our civilization rushes on at lightning speed, he must not expect
that the melancholy fact will altogether escape the
knowledge of his former associates.

If the Committee really wish to inquire into the educative effect of our shop-work let them examine it carefully in view of its primary object as I have stated it
above, and then see whether the mastery sought is generally worth gaining; whether there is a more efficient
method of gaining it; whether our pupils really achieve
it; and what its real educational influence is.

VI.

INTELLECTUAL POWERS, MISCHIEVOUS, BENEFICIAL AND OTHERWISE.

I come now to a most remarkable sample of argu-
mentation.

The Report says:—

" Your committee would here call attention to other
arguments often used which are weak and misleading;
such, for example, as the statement that manual training cultivates the powers of attention, perseverance,
and industry. These are formal powers and not substantial; that is to say, they derive their value from
what they are applied to, and they may be mischievous
as well as beneficial. The power of attention may be
cultivated by the game of chess, or the game of whist,
or of draw poker, or to [sic] the picking of pockets;
but it is only attention to those subjects, and not attention in general that is cultivated."

In a similar vein, reference is made to games of
" marbles, quoits, base-ball and jack-straws. These

too are educative, as manual training is, in the powers
named; and they carry with them some general training." "But it would not be fair to expect that these
qualities of mind would show themselves in the boys'
work in mathematics or history."

It must not be supposed that there is any argument
in the above, and I do not suppose that any member of
the Committee would claim that there is.   The fact
that a game is or is not educative does not prove that
grammar and wood-turning are or are not educative.
Nevertheless, there appears to be an attempt to belittle
manual training by coupling it with games.   The sug-
gestion of a "*mischievous power of attention*" is cer-
tainly an original one; but the subsequent illustrations
of gamblers, pick-pockets, and dynamiters, are scarcely
graceful or in good taste.   If they have any force at
all in the discussion, it is to the effect that the influence
of manual training in cultivating attention, perseverance,
industry, dexterity, and accuracy may not only be not
good, but positively bad.

But the propriety of calling the powers of attention,
perseverance and industry, "*beneficial powers*" or "*mischievous powers*," I most seriously question.   One may
be *attentive* to things good or evil; one may *persevere*
in right-doing or in wrong-doing; one may be *indus-
trious* in useful or harmful work; but that a committee
of four eminent psychologists should soberly assert that
these intellectual *powers* can be good or bad, beneficial
or mischievous, is passing strange !

A little later in the Report the Committee appear to
lament the unwillingness of manual training people to
insist upon the repetition of exercises in shop-work till
all interest is gone, and till the work excites disgust;

because, by such refusal an educative opportunity is lost; "for the patience and perseverance that pursues its work to the end, and bravely keeps down any tendencies to disgust at the lack of novelty, is a moral education indispensable to success in any manual calling."

Are not the powers [or habits] of patience and perseverance just as "formal" and non-"substantial" as ever? and are the Committee sure that here they are beneficial and not mischievous? May not a pick-pocket be patient? and a dynamiter be persevering?

Moreover, when can one know that he is cultivating "attention in general?" Whenever one gives attention to anything it is always to something in particular, not something in general. The committee twice mention approvingly the study of grammar. Perhaps grammar is sufficiently something in general and nothing in particular to be capable of cultivating "attention in general."

Again, is it not just possible that there may be something "mischievous" in the power of attention to certain book-learning, as shown by the tendency of bookish people to dislike manual labor, and sometimes even to become bad citizens — not to mention dynamiters?

One more word in regard to the educative opportunity lost by not requiring pupils to overcome the tendency to disgust at lack of novelty. The Report says:—

"No teaching in the studies of the school as they are would be esteemed of a high order if it did not train its pupils to attack difficult studies and courageously overcome them. Mere natural disinclination and impatience must be conquered before the child can become a rational being."

Now the two cases are in no wise parallel. When pupils feel a repugnance to attack difficult studies we urge them to persist, for we know that there is something there which will reward effort. When success does come there is plenty of novelty, and the "habit of doing" is strengthened by the result, which is the mastery of a difficult study.

But when one repeats many times an exercise from which all educative juice has been extracted, he has nothing to reward his effort. The longer he works the less he gets, and disgust is not only natural but highly proper. No amount of trying can overcome it, and the longer one is kept at it the more intense the disgust, unless, perchance, he falls into that unhappy, stupid condition in which one is willing to repeat indefinitely a senseless and fruitless operation.

"Natural disinclination" to do useless things is to be respected, and should never be conquered. Laziness, physical and mental, should be conquered, and the love of study, whether with book, tool or apparatus, should be stimulated by a reasonable hope of something to recompense earnest effort. Legitimate manual work is not without its opportunities for promoting industry and encouraging hard work, but the repetition of empty exercises is not one of them.

It may, perhaps, be replied to this that students of the school may become actual mechanics or routine workers in after life, and that as such they will be obliged to repeat many processes from which all lively interest will long since have disappeared, yet they must keep on, with or without disgust.

To this it should at once be answered that the all-sufficient motive then will be, not novelty, not ideas and principles, but wages. Every stroke of work will then mean money, and every repetition will mean more money. Attention will be shifted to a new object which has perpetual interest. No such pecuniary interest comes into school work.

Dr. S. H. Peabody, of Illinois, endeavored to re-enforce the argument of the Repórt in his paper read at Nashville the day after the Report was made. He said, after referring to the passage quoted above : —

"Accuracy, for example, is of first importance, and no tool-work that fails to show it in a reasonable and constantly refining degree ought for an instant tó be tolerated. But accuracy, nakedly and without relationship, has no ethical quality. Accuracy and truth are not synonyms. *Accuracy is good or evil according to its purpose.* Accuracy in fitting a jimmy, that may be used for house-breaking, means burglary. Accurate pistol practice, on the night before a duel, means murder. In like manner, industry is good or evil according to its relationship."

Is there not something chaotic in all that ? He declares that accuracy is of first importance, nothing short of it should be for an instant tolerated. So say we, and we claim that manual work is peculiarly favorable to the acquisition of habits of accuracy and industry. Whereupon he wheels square round and declares that there is nothing ethical in naked accuracy. Accuracy and industry may both be evil. Accuracy may mean burglary or murder!

I hope we may not claim too much for manual training. I do not wish to say that there is in it anything which on fair trial will not be found there. It is *not* a panacea for all evils, social, domestic, or personal. It has no monopoly of educational values. It has not even a corner on good habits. It is a valuable educational feature, and should stand beside other valuable educational features, and be judged, as they are, by its fruits. I protest that there is no just excuse for dragging into this discussion burglars, murderers and dynamiters, as though they in some way furnished arguments against manual training. As to the ethical quality of "accuracy without relationship," I think I shall decline to agree. A single remark must however suffice. When a boy has actually acquired habits of accuracy, attention, perseverance and industry, in a manual training school or in any other good school, his naked chance of becoming a burglar, a murderer or a dynamiter is diminished fully ninety-five per cent.

One is led to ask if the Committee ever thought of applying their method of reasoning to other branches than manual training. Let them try arithmetic, for example. The Report quotes M. Sluys to the effect "that when the child is compelled to manufacture large numbers of a given object in order to acquire skill in the work, the educative value of the work diminishes. 'From the third or fourth sample his interest wanes; mechanical repetition invariably excites disgust for the work.'"

The failure of manual training schools to force pupils on to the point of disgust constitutes the "opportunity lost." Now, suppose we apply the same reasoning, thus :—

When the child is compelled to perform large numbers of examples in Long Division in order to acquire skill in

*the work, the educative value of the work. diminishes.
From the third or fourth page of such examples his interest wanes; mechanical repetition invariably excites disgust in the work.*

Keep that work up for fifty or sixty solid pages, with
a view to acquiring the skill of a lightning calculator,
and there will be " disgust " enough for an entire moral
education.

This attempt to make a point against the method of
manual training on account of the " opportunity lost "
seems to involve the Committee in some confusion.   In
order to give validity to another argument it was necessary to assume that the shop-work was " trade work,"
with endless repetitions, until freedom of action was
lost in muscular stiffness and insensibility.

The Committee declare that it is a fact that such repetitions are " deadening to the mind." — But " the
advocates of manual training admit " this fact, and consequently avoid such repetitions as contrary to the theory of the school.   They steer wide of trade methods
and trade-work. — " This, of course," the Report says,
" makes against the economical argument," but it must
not be allowed to stand in favor of the methods of the
manual training schools as they exist ; so the Committee
brings in this argument of an " educative opportunity .
lost."   One is reminded of the children in the market
place.*

---

* Vide Matth. xi : 16–19.

VII.

THE ECONOMIC VALUE OF THE METHOD OF MANUAL TRAINING.

Does the method of the manual training school "make against the economic argument" in behalf of such schools?

The Report says: —

" The advocates of manual training admit that it is useful as education only if not carried to the point of arriving at skill in production. This feature, of course, makes against the economical argument in behalf of such schools. According to the economic view, skill in production is the primary object aimed at by introducing the training of the hand into schools."

I could well afford to pass this attempt to array against manual training those who advocate trade instruction and trade schools. I do not know how many of such men there are among us. I have never met ten in my whole experience, and those I have met were outside the schools and confessedly unfamiliar with the details of either trades or schools. Nevertheless, I should be sorry to have any one misled by such an argument. I shall therefore try to show that the refusal . on the part of the teacher of manual training to adopt " factory " methods, and insist upon repetitions until motions become semi-automatic, requiring little or no conscious mental activity, does *not* "make against the economic argument."

The highest economy in all arts and all industries is that which most employs brains. If there be any art or industry which is not more remunerative the more one brings to it intellectual training of a healthy sort, let us boycott it. One's value in whatever manly occupation is in proportion to his intelligence, his potential energy (to borrow a term from mechanics), and that energy depends upon the amount of intellectual power at his command. What we call *skill* in executive work depends upon speed, order and accuracy. When the mind has mastered the conditions of order and accuracy, the major part of skill has been achieved.* Speed comes with practice, in which there is scarcely a new idea. Again, if, the moment one has grasped the conditions of order and accuracy as related to the material to be wrought, the tools to be used, and the forms to be produced, — he sets out by numerous repetitions to acquire the element of speed which shall combine with the former to produce skill, he loses numerous opportunities to acquire an intelligent mastery of other materials, processes, and conditions. The student who stops to acquire complete skill, narrows his training and shuts himself out of the range of free activity. The lack of true economy in such a course seems plain. Hence, while a manual training school aims not at complete skill in individual operations, it does aim at the intellectual part of all operations. I am as certain as I can be of anything not actually tested by experience, that the manual training school would have far less economic value of it should cease to make intellectual training its chief object, and set about producing skillful factory hands and producing articles for the market.

---

* Bacon said that what he had been able to accomplish was due to "order and method."

Let no one be surprised that I speak thus of intellectual training ; that I set it forward as the pre-eminent object of a manual training school.   There is no royal road to intellectual power.   Perception, memory, imagination and judgment may be cultivated in a thousand ways.   When one sets out to select the best means for training the intellect and the will he is embarrassed by the great variety of available appliances.   Generally, extraneous considerations determine his choice.   He is governed largely by convenience and the incidental value of what the mind, stores up and exercises itself upon.   It would be very easy to show that convenience, availability, use, conventionality and fashion have largely shaped the traditional course of study.   By fashion I include an active tendency away from utilitarian ends to such a degree that the purely intellectual value of a study is held to increase as its practical value decreases.   In other words, it is the fashion to assume that, if a study has no economic value, its intellectual value must be not only pure but great.   This doctrine must be admitted as partly true.   If a study has no economic value, its value must be purely intellectual, whatever that may be — there is no denying that conclusion; but it does not at all follow that because its value is wholly intellectual, it is therefore greater than the intellectual value of another study, which is at the same time very useful.   Herein lies a very weak point in the position of those who oppose the introduction of manual training on what they call educational grounds. They talk loudly about intellectual studies, * and stoutly

* The Report uses the word "spiritual" and "spiritual education" repeatedly, as if the word furnished a stronger contrast with the "gross materialism" of manual training.

maintain their superiority to mere manual exercises which have only low and sordid ends.

If they are "*mere*" manual exercises, such a statement is of course sound, and is trite enough, but when these opponents go on to draw conclusions from it adverse to manual training, their error is twofold. First, they ignore the fact that manual *studies* are intellectual as well as manual; and secondly, they fail to take account of the fact that the intellectual elements involved in them are for the most part of a very superior character, admirably suited to stimulate and invigorate the mental faculties.

I am anxious not to misrepresent those who fail to agree with us. They honestly believe that it injures the educative influence of a study to have a clear and decided practical bearing. They have often claimed that its tendency is to corrupt the mind; to withdraw the attention and interest from purely intellectual ends; to lower the moral tone. If improperly taught, it may be so, as one may study pedagogics from sordid motives, and hence we cannot take too great pains to secure a quality and manner of teaching which is of the highest grade. Nothing is more fatal and disappointing than ignorant and ill-trained teachers.

But with competent and thoroughly trained teachers the supposed demoralizing influence of the practical side of a study does not occur. The question of what is moral, what intellectual, and what practical in a study does not rise particularly in the minds of pupils. Every study should bear in all three directions. No sensible teacher ever says to his pupils (what no one should ever be *able* to say), " This study has no practical value, but it is highly intellectual." On the contrary, every good teacher aims to impress his pupils with the immense probable and possible practical value of a complete mastery of the subject in hand. The best intellectual culture is gained unconsciously, when the student is so absorbed in his work that he takes no thought of its effect upon himself. On the other hand, how absolutely unhealthy is the effect, both morally and intellectually, of a study, a book, or an exercise which a student hates and shirks, and is glad to lay aside forever! The traditional curriculum for secondary schools has been so pruned and trimmed in order that the economic may be at a minimum, and the purely intellectual (*i.e.*, the practically useless) may be at a maximum, that the pupils who are keenly alive to the . necessity of practical training, and parents who feel as the Supt. Sabin of Iowa puts it, that only " applied (appliable) knowledge is power," see little beyond the three R's which to the average youth is worth the getting.

Paradoxical as it may seem to many, manual training was organized and is carried on in the interest of a better and more rational intellectual training. It aims alike and at the same time to intellectual culture, to moral worth, and at practical power and efficiency.

VIII.

THE ARGUMENT AGAINST LIBERAL CULTURE IN TOOL-WORK.

The last argument against manual training urged by the Report is a purely economic one and very wide of the mark at that; and hence might well be overlooked,

but it has appeared so frequently and so persistently —
it appeared three times at Nashville in three different
papers— that it may be well to attempt to dispose of
it now for good. The Report says:—

" The education of the muscles of the hand and arm,
the training of the eye in accuracy, go for something in
the way of education, especially if these, too, are of a
general character, and productive of skill in many arts.
But it happens in most cases that the training of the
muscles for a special operation unfits it more or less
for the other special operations. Every trade has its
special knack or skill, and not only requires special
education to fit the laborer to pursue it, but it reacts on
him, and fixes in his bodily organism certain limitations
which for greater or less extent unfit him for other
occupations. The work of blacksmithing, for instance,
would unfit one for engraving; the work in planing and
sawing would diminish the skill of the wood-carver.
Work in the trades that deal with wood and metals
(and these include the entire curriculum of the manual
training school) would be disadvantageous to the delicate touch required by the laborer on textile manufactures; and this class of laborers is nearly as large as
the combined classes of wood and metal workers."

In the discussion which followed the reading of the
Report, Dr. Harris explained that by the "delicate
touch required by the laborer on textile manufactures,"
he meant such things as "picking up threads and tying
knots."

So many ideas struggle for expression in comment-
ing on that paragraph that I scarcely know where to
begin. It must be perfectly transparent to all that the
writer could not have been thinking much of the work
actually done in manual training schools. He was
thinking of trades and trade-work all the time, calcu-

lating the number of wood-workers, metal-workers and textile-workers in the United States, and supposing that the mastery of one trade unfits for another.

Unless manual training is trade training, the passage has no force in the Report. On no purely educational theory does the number of laborers in a certain class, as shown by the census, have claim to consideration. As the manual training school is *not* a trade school, either in theory or practice, I might dismiss the matter as irrelevant, but were I to do so, I might appear to admit that the economic value of tool-training, even when carried to a point far short of the demands of a trade, was diminished by giving it breadth and liberality.

Now we do not doubt that a fair proportion of our students will become mechanics. Students from high schools which do not have manual training, become mechanics and why should not ours? All of our students have high respect for mechanical skill; without exception they all enjoy shop-work; and the demand for our students from manufacturers is very great. What wonder then if many find it for their interest to accept positions as tool-users?

Let me warn the reader not to be misled by shallow reasoning on this point. If one does not become or remain a mechanic it does not prove that he dislikes manual work; it only suggests that he has found some other occupation more remunerative. On the other hand it does not follow that because one does become a mechanic he is therefore in love with manual labor. People are often forced to perform labor which they hate. Examples have not been wanting in recent educational literature, in which writers have reasoned very weakly on these points.

Returning now to our examination of the passage from the Report, in spite of its extravagant trade bias, and an insinuation that our training is too narrow, we find a distinct argument that it is too broad. The argument as it applies to us stands as follows: Long practice in special narrow operations results in certain muscular habits which seriously interfere with one's free activity when he would undertake different operations. What is true for long practice is proportionately true for short practice; hence, what one acquires at the forge unfits him for the joiner's bench, and conversely; an exercise which hardens one's hands disqualifies for an exercise requiring soft and flexible fingers.

Such appears to be the argument, — purely muscular and physical in character. I do not understand that there is any claim of mental disqualification, — and yet it seems to me that there ought to be, for it is there that is found the most unfortunate effect of endless repetitions of muscular operations. Stupidity is the fate of Mr. Brown's turner of plow-handles. " Ten hours a day for twenty years has transformed the man into a machine." His work demands no conscious effort of the mind, and hence the mind lies idle while the hands move automatically. It is possible that such a mind may become so blunted and deadened that healthy mental activity is impossible. Such would be the argument of the Report if it consistently made the most of its position.

Now, let us see how these theories — including the one I have added to make them consistent and complete on the supposition of long, unbroken practice, — apply to such work as is really under discussion, viz.: the tool-work of the manual training school.

To begin with, the law of simple, direct or inverse proportion does not hold in measuring the intensity of mental activity in the act of repeating a special operation or exercise. A man may become dull and insensible, mentally and physically, while repeating the same special operation three million times, but it does not follow that he would grow dull and insensible to the one-millionth of the former extent, as the result of repeating the operation three times. If the operation were one requiring skill, with the elements of order, accuracy and speed, the probability is that the interest and the mental activity would increase gradually to a maximum and then begin to wane. So long as the art was imperfectly understood, so long as it stood as a challenge to one's intelligence, the interest would grow. As soon, however, as the intellectual part of the art was mastered, and nothing remained but the necessity of a more perfect co-ordination of the muscles to produce speed, the interest would rapidly fall away.

This may be clearly represented by a diagram.

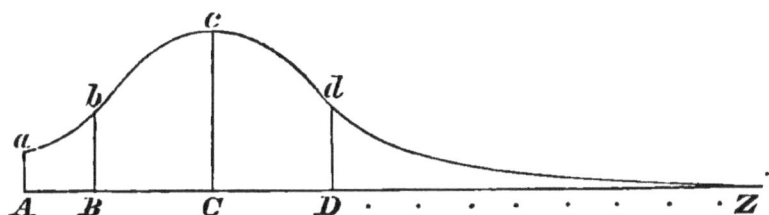

Let the line A B C . . . Z denote the lapse of time required for countless repetitions of a special operation. Let the perpendiculars Aa Bb Cc, &c., denote the degrees of interest which mark the mental activity during different repetitions. The initial interest Aa may be greater or less; if the exercise is well chosen, the interest will increase slowly at first, then rapidly as at Bb. The number of repetitions required to reach

5

the maximum Cc varies greatly with the nature and complexity of the operation, but the time is sure to come earlier or later when the mental characteristic of the exercise diminishes; this is shown by a waning interest.

In a *school*, the repetition is never carried far into this waning period. Every special operation should be laid aside for a new one the moment the mental activity has fairly passed its maximum. The intellectual part of the exercise has been mastered and hence that special exercise should cease. No good teacher would carry it beyond Dd. When the mental condition indicated by Dd has been reached, in the place of a lively interest there is a keen sense of satisfaction. The feeling is precisely akin to that with which one rises from an intelligent mastery of a new subject in algebra or a poem of Browning. The argument in the Report seems to be based upon the assumption that the repetitions are carried on till the point Z is reached, the region of mental insensibility, *sans* interest, *sans* profit, *sans* everything. The reader will now see, if he did not before, the force of my remark that the intensity of mental activity and growth is not determined by simple proportion. It is seen that there is a tide in the intellectual activity of students, whatever may be the matter in hand, and it is the important duty of the teacher to know when it is at its flood. A growing interest and zeal is contagious and so is a waning one. Beware the ebbing tide.

The application of this mental analysis to the argument of the Report is easy. So long as we go not beyond the point of lively interest, we go not into the realm of unconscious activity. Every movement is determined by the conscious will, not by habit. No automatism has set in, and consequently every motion

may be modified without the necessity of breaking up
a muscular habit, for no such habit has been formed.
The hand exerts much force or little as the mind wills,
with equal facility. The watch-maker's hammer or the
blacksmith's sledge is handled without interference and
with equal interest so long as equal directive intelligence is required. There is more in either than was at
first suspected, but what one finds in mastering the tiny
hammer is no hindrance to mastering what is to be
found in the manipulation of the massive sledge. On
the other hand one is a positive preparation for the
other. The mental activities are in part identical, and
the physical activities differ more in degree than in
kind. Consequently the thorough mastery of the one
process renders the mastery of the other an easy matter.
Hence related exercises of that sort should not appear
too numerously in the manual training curriculum. It
would be educationally wasteful to bring in exercises
with all the hammers, — those of the silversmith, the carpenter, the machinist, the forge-worker, the shoemaker,
and the stone-mason — because having mastered some,
the mastery of the others is so easy that their educational value is insufficient; the time and opportunity
can be more profitably spent on wholly new ground.

I said that the mental activities were *in part* identical,
and I have shown that so far as they are identical a new
analogous operation is more easy and proportionally
less valuable educationally. But the activities are in
part dissimilar, in consequence of new materials and
new conditions. Hence a liberal range must be allowed
that the judgment may be broadly trained, and that the
mind may be led to make critical comparisons. Hence
in manual training schools, from Massachusetts to Cal-

ifornia, and from Minnesota to Louisiana, hammers are used—(I keep in mind the use of hammers as an illustration, partly because the hammer has, so to speak, been so often thrown at us, and partly because it may well be taken as typical of numerous classes of tools)—hammers are used on tiny brads and on huge spikes, in mortising and in wood-carving (*i.e.*, wooden hammers or mallets), on soft and hard iron (hot and cold), on lead and on steel. This is liberal culture, reasonably sufficient for both for mental discipline and for rigid economy.

But I am not limited to psychological reasoning in establishing the value of a' liberal culture. There is abundant evidence from actual experience that neither in the manual training school nor in the realm of practical mechanics is it found that skill (such as there may be), with one set of tools, stands in the way of acquiring skill with different tools.

If I am not mistaken, President Peabody, of the Illinois University, whom I have already quoted, first suggested the argument which appears in the Report. More explicitly, he asserted that the ability to use correctly the carpenter's hammer is not only of no value in learning to use a machinist's hammer, but that it is a positive hindrance; in other words, that it is more difficult to make a machinist out of a carpenter, or a carpenter out of a machinist, than it is to make a carpenter or a machinist out of a green hand who never handled a hammer of any sort. Says he, "if the one use of a hammer which the boy has acquired, does not interfere with the use of it in a different way or for a different purpose, then I much doubt whether he has really learned that one use." I suppose Dr. Peabody has a

standard of attainment in hammering peculiarly his
own, for he goes on to add : "Certain kinds of skill
require that a man stop thinking, and put himself as
nearly as possible in the condition of a machine and
carry through a series of movements like a machine."
I have no use for men nor for boys who have reached
that stage. All persons I meet have abundant and
continual use for their brains.

Not long since it became necessary for our teacher of
metal work to take a class in joinery and wood-turning.
He had learned the machinists' trade and had been at work
on iron and steel for ten or fifteen years, and no one pre-
sumed to say that he had not "really learned" the use
of the metal-working tools. He was a comparative
stranger to joinery and knew absolutely nothing about
wood-turning. It was astonishing to see how quickly
he mastered the new tools. In a dozen lessons he
learned more than a green hand, who had never used
tools at all, would have learned in fifty lessons. So boys
who come to our school with some knowledge of iron
work *always* go to the front in wood work. And boys
who enter the school in advance of the regular admission, and who consequently lack the tool training of the
earlier year or years, are always at great disadvantage
in shop-work, though the operations omitted are quite
unlike those they enter upon.

I have made systematic study of this question, with
the results as stated. There is not a shop teacher in
my school who does not hold that this "unfitting" argument is totally unsound. In my Harvard days I was
an oarsman for three years, and I know well the degree of stiffness and insensibility which the automatism
of daily pulling a long oar gives to one's hands. There

is nothing in the whole course of tool-work in a manual training school which can be compared with rowing in that regard. Last year two of my graduating students were unusually skillful musicians, one on the piano, the other on the violin. Neither ever complained of stiff fingers, though one of them said the iron work soiled his hands and spoiled his nails. Those, however, were trifling matters which a week's vacation would remove.

Here I submit the arguments. The position of the Report appears to me to be unsound, whether examined *a priori* or *a posteriori*. My conclusion is that knowledge, intelligence, skill, power and culture are always helpful in the acquisition of more knowledge, more intelligence, more skill, more power, and more culture. The more accomplished one is, the easier new things are to him, whether in the realm of pure intellect or in the field where mind and hand are cultivated together.

IX.

CONCLUSION.

The significant report of Supt. Seaver, of Boston, touching the "educative value" of manual training is a timely commentary on this Council Report. Mr. Seaver's report, which accompanies his plan for a complete Manual Training High School for the City of Boston, is so *apropos* that I venture to give a generous quotation. He was commissioned to visit the manual training schools of Chicago, Toledo, Cleveland, Baltimore, Philadelphia and St. Louis, and to make a thorough inspection. Of one of his visits he speaks as follows :—

"The Director of the school bade me make myself perfectly at home, question the teachers, question the boys, and make my investigation as thorough as was in my power with all the help they could give. I devoted four days to the investigation. The results were a large book full of notes, and a clear impression in my mind of a well-organized and vigorously working school. I cannot here go into details. Suffice it to say, I used my privilege of questioning freely and thoroughly. I followed classes from the school-rooms into the drawing-rooms, and into the shops. I found the boys equally alert and intelligent in all branches of their work. They were as ready to describe and give the reasons for every step in the process of forging a pair of blacksmith's tongs, as they were to state and give the reasons for every step in the demonstration of a geometrical theorem. There are those who doubt the 'educative value' of manual training. Let any such person spend a few hours in a good manual training school, like this, observing the boys at their work and questioning them about it; and if his doubts about the 'educative value' of manual training do not vanish, it will be because he measures 'educative value' by standards not in common use. I should desire him particularly to converse with those boys in the machine-shop, now drawing near the close of their school course, and busily at work on their 'projects' for graduation day. Let him ask for explanations, question them closely for reasons, observe the quality of their work, note their own criticisms and estimates of it, and he must be an unreasonable man if he does not admit that somehow their school training has developed in them a high degree of intelligence. The result is too striking to be overlooked, analyze and account for it as we may." *

As a companion to the above from the superintendent of the public schools of Boston, I venture to insert

* See School Document, No. 15, 1889, City of Boston.

an extract from the last report of Superintendent Mac-Alister, of the public schools of Philadelphia.

He says that while the courses in tool-work and drawing are the distinctive features of the manual training school, " it must be borne in mind that the others are not neglected. On account of its novelty the manual training is apt to make the strongest impression upon visitors, and they do not always discover that the literary and scientific training are just as fully recognized and provided for. Anything like a one-sided culture is carefully avoided, the aim of the school being to give to each branch, whether scholastic or manual, such relative importance as shall lead to a fuller and more symmetrical development of mind and body than has been possible under the old systems of secondary education.

"The success which has attended the manual training school from the first is the best guarantee of the soundness of the principles upon which it is organized and conducted. Beginning a little more than four years ago, in a very humble way, it has steadily grown in public confidence and approval. *It has more than justified every claim that was made in its behalf. Every available foot of space is now occupied, and it has now become impossible to admit all the pupils who apply for admission.* The Board of Education has therefore been brought face to face with the question whether the time has not come for opening another manual training school in such a quarter of the city as may be deemed most advantageous to the public interests. The original intention of the Board was to establish four or five of these schools as fast as a just regard for the other departments of the school system would permit, and the growing demand for the kind of education which this school represents will render the fulfillment of this purpose a necessity at no very remote date." *

[The italics in the above extract are mine.]

---

* Manual training in the Public Schools of Philadelphia, by James MacAlister, Superintendent, March, 1890.

Thus the work goes on. The intellectual fruits of a rational, well-proportioned system of manual training are so evident to every close observer and student of that training that I am sorry that the Committee are unable to see them. Manual training will go on all the same, and I hope that every member of the Committee will live to see that, far from being a power for mischief, it is a potent instrumentality for good ; that it is a strong and friendly ally in promoting educational progress, and in ameliorating the condition of all classes of our people. I earnestly hope that manual training may be able to contribute something to bring about that splendid consummation, eloquently pictured by Geo. Wm. Curtis, when " with one hand education shall lead the young American to the secrets of material skill, and equip him to enter into the fullest trade with all the world; but with the other it shall lead him to lofty thoughts and to commerce with the skies."

A CRITICAL REVIEW OF THE REPORT OF THE COMMITTEE ON PEDAGOGICS.

BY GILBERT B. MORRISON.

The National Teachers'. Association, which held its last session at Nashville, Tenn., revealed some interesting and peculiar characteristics. Of the subjects discussed the most important was that of manual training. To those who believe that an education means more than an "abnormal tumefying of the inner consciousness," it was gratifying to see that the programme of this National Convention of Teachers gave a place to the discussion of manual training. Still more would it seem to the disinterested spectator that more than a passing deference was being shown this phase of school work, from the fact that it was made the subject of the labors of the Committee on Pedagogics. But to these first impressions of professional countenance the report itself furnishes a curious contradiction.

I wish it to be understood at the outset, that I shall try to treat this report solely on its merits, regardless of the known ability of the committee in general, and Professor Harris in particular, for whom I have great admiration and respect; and it is, perhaps, the heightened expectation accompanying admiration which makes this report seem to me somewhat disappointing.

To a citizen of the nation, who has a right to expect from a committee representing national interests an unbiased report of a painstaking investigation of the

(60)

facts and principles involved, the following from the prelude, which seems to be an apology for considering the question at all, is interesting : —

" This subject has come to be of prime importance, by reason of the strong claims set up for it by its advocates, and secondly, by reason of the fact that as a cause it serves to unite, not only the critics of the educational system already existing, but also its uncompromising enemies; thirdly, because the claims set forth in its behalf are based, not on economic reasons but on educational reasons, an assumption being actually made that the effect of manual training on the pupil is educational in the same sense as the branches of science and literature heretofore taught, or at least if different from them, of equal or of superior value to them. This assumption unsettles the entire question of course of study, in so far as it rests on the doctrine of a specific educational value for each of the branches of the course of study, and in so far as it is supposed that the present list of branches provides for an all-sided intellectual training."

When this prelude was read, I thought it might be expressed in fewer words, somewhat as follows : " The system of public education in this country rests on a ' doctrine.' That doctrine does not include manual training. That doctrine is settled. Manual training would ' unsettle ' it. The ' advocates ' of manual training even claim that it has pure educational value. They are therefore enemies to the present educational system. But they are making a great deal of noise, and we, the committee, will now proceed to give the presumptuous intruders a black eye from the fist of high authority."

The discussion which followed the reading of the report would remove any doubt of the justice of my paraphrase of it. The council, with surprising energy and alacrity, rallied almost unanimously to the support of the statements expressed in the report. · Professor C. M. Woodward, of St. Louis, seemed to be alone in the defense of manual training. But his solitude was only apparent. Others present would have joined their voices with his had not the ruling of the council silenced them. Only members of the council were allowed to be heard. I could not help reflecting that it would take something more than membership, however honorable, to demonstrate the fitness of the remarks of many who spoke on this question.

Listening to these venerable schoolmasters discussing manual training schools, persistently calling them "trade schools," trying to measure them by their own individual experience and preconceived notions, reminded me of the following anecdote :—

An aged hunter, who in his young days had been considered a " dead shot," was accustomed to sit by his fireside, an old-fashioned chimney-place, looking reverently at his old and trusty flint-lock, which he never allowed to be removed from his sight. One beautiful day in early spring, the sun shining through an open window, fell upon the shaggy brow and silvery hair of the veteran. Its genial warmth seemed to revive in him something of his youthful vigor. Peering wistfully out, he discovered a squirrel frisking in a neighboring tree. With the unerring instinct of habit he seized his gun—still sitting in his chair—took aim and fired. He then sat calmly waiting for his son, who was working in the garden, to bring in the coveted rodent. When the smoke had cleared away he saw, to his surprise and chagrin, the same squirrel still sporting with undisturbed equanimity in the same tree. The old man summoned all his energy, re-loaded his gun, took a more careful aim, and fired again. To his now un-disguised amazement the squirrel still remained. The son had by this time arrived, in haste to learn the meaning of this in-door musketry. Looking into the anxious and troubled face of his aged parent, he at once discovered the situation, and exclaimed: " Why, pa, dear pa, there is a parasite (*Pediculous capitis*) on your eyelash! "

The educational leaders of the United States seem to be shooting at an illusion, which they call the " trade school." But the manual training school, which is to them only another name for the same thing, still con-tinues to sport in the upper branches of public favor after the smoke of each pedagogical volley has cleared away.

Quoting again from the report:—

" Your committee, accordingly, have proposed to themselves in this report to discuss the various phases of this *assumption*, and to inquire in what precisely consists the educational functions of the branches taught in the manual training school."

The committee here assume that the claims of manual training rest on an " assumption ; " they there-fore do not deem it part of their duty to examine the schools themselves, but only to draw from their inner consciousness arguments to refute the "assumption."

Again :—

" They (the committee) have proposed to treat inci-dentally, also, the economic questions involved, inas-

much as the popularity of the movement has its
foundation in the conviction that if the schools teach
manual training, all pupils will be fitted for useful industries before the age of leaving school for business."

Is this not an admission that there is a popular be-
lief that the schools as now existing do *not* fit the
pupils for useful industries, and therefore do not give
that "all-sided" training which is claimed for them?
There could hardly be better evidence that the schools
as now existing are not wholly satisfactory, than that a
proposed change is popular, even though untried and
opposed by the pedagogical cult of the nation.

The committee now go out of their way to discuss
"special trade" schools, and admit that the training
furnished by them is superior to the old apprentice
system. "But," say they, "your committee insists
that such manual training ought not to be begun before the completion of the twelfth year of the pupil."
This is another shot at the supposed squirrel, and has
no application to manual training schools as now existing, which are simply high schools with the manual
element incorporated.

But it might be well to stop here to reflect on the un-
soundness of the statement that manual training should
not begin before the twelfth year. Manual training
means using the hands, as intellectual training means
using the mind. And the former is essential to the
normal use of the latter. Children learn more during
the first five years of their life than during any subsequent five years. This is because they have more
manual exercise during this period. They use their
little hands continually, finding out the properties of
matter, enjoying that reflex activity between the brain

and sensorium, which is one of the fundamental conditions of correct thinking. Frœbel recognized this principle when he founded the kindergarten, which is nothing more than juvenile manual training. The fault of educational systems is that this manual training, or what might otherwise be called normal intellectual training, does not continue. In the stereotyped American school the pupil must stop this " play," form in line outside the school-house, march in when the teacher taps the bell, fold his hands that they may do no " mischief," toe the mark, and learn to read and spell. Read and spell what? Words, words, words! which often mean nothing to him. But it is done in good " form," and therefore supposed to be "all-sided." Frœbel has done good service for primary grades, Professor Woodward and others for high school grades, and he who shall devise a system of manual training applicable to the intermediate and grammar grades, will do a service equal in value to either of these.

The Report continues: " Your committee understand that any amount of manual training conducted in a school is no equivalent for the school education in letters and science, and ought not to be substituted for it." This implies that when manual training begins, education in science, etc., ends. This is a somewhat strange doctrine in this age of experimental and applied science, wherein the manual element is an organic and indispensable part of the work. This committee does not appear to be aware that science cannot be learned without the manual element. They evidently belong to that school of educators who believe that science can be learned historically. They believe in reading *on* science instead of working *in* science. Who ever knew a scientist worthy of the name who was not an experimenter? Encyclopedic information about things does not furnish correct conceptions of those things. With all active men of science the manual element is uppermost; and forms the fundamental condition of correct concepts. Every experimental laboratory wherein the pupils are allowed to work is a manual training school. The student in a manual training school proper, uses his tools as the student of science uses his apparatus, chiefly as the necessary means in forming correct ideas.

The educational bias which ignores the manual element in education is difficult to account for. It is the bias which possesses that class which, as Colonel Garrick Mallory expresses it, regards him the best teacher "who has most enormously tumefied his inner consciousness, and who can then expose its morbidity by the most pretentious diagnosis."

The intimation in this report that manual training is unfavorable to the study of science, must be amusing to any one who has had any experience in science-teaching. An experience of ten years in teaching physics and chemistry is sufficient to convince me that manual training is indispensable to the proper pursuit of these studies. The boy from the farm or shop will always outstrip the boy who has never stooped to the "vulgar" material. Pupils who come to the High School from the Grammar School are mere infants when taken to an experiment, and away from their shadows of ideas — words. The time spent with them must therefore be of the most rudimentary character — such as teaching them how to observe, how to exercise their senses, and to interpret impressions. The true nature

of the work done in the average Grammar School can
be seen by the persistency with which the student turns
from the examination and discussion of *things*, and the
alacrity with which he seizes and retains words which
are supposed to represent things.

"Physical maturity is necessary to the formation of
the best muscular movements to produce skill," say the
committee. Why not also say, " Mental maturity is
necessary to the formation of the best mental movements to produce thought." This is much like saying,
" Do not begin to climb the hill till you get to the top."
It is saying to the young fledgeling, " Do not try to fly
until you have risen above the housetops, for the objects below would impede ' freedom of movement.' "

The time-prescription method by which learned educators pretend to assign work specially adapted to each
year of a child's life, and that of a different character
from that which preceded it, is artificial and stultifying.
Healthy growth results from healthy natural exercise
of mind and body. The exercise need not differ in its
nature at different periods. It varies only in degree
both as to quantity and quality.

Science, language, etc., are simply thought and its
expression, and can be as easily taught to a child of
eight years as to the senior in college. The young
child begins with his playthings to study the nature of
things, and his first words and sentences are expressions
of his thoughts. The college senior, if his work is
what it should be, is but continuing the process. His
investigations in science are but the continuation of his
study into the nature of things. The discovery of a
child that fire burns, and that it will destroy his toy if
he expose it, is of the same nature, so far as thought

5

processes are concerned, as the discovery by his father
that a certain amalgam will melt at 250°, and will therefore serve a useful purpose as a safety plug or electric
light cut-off. With the boy who has run away from his
geography lesson, and while building a dam across the
brook finds that sand and ordinary mud will not do,
and then seeks clay, it is not different in nature from
the work of the student in studying the strength of
materials in mechanical engineering. If the young
dam-builder were led to write his essay on his engineering efforts, how would it differ in nature or mental
process from the effort of the senior in preparing his
thesis? When reading his juvenile stories, character-
izing some as funny, some sad, and exercising his
powers in similar efforts of his own, he is studying
what he will later, when analyzing Shakespeare, call
literature. It is only the conventional " doctrine" of
time-prescription which is equal to the task of starting
off the memory at one time, the reason at another, the
observation at another, and manual exercise at another,
gravely asserting that " the industrial school should
not be allowed to take possession of the youth until the
completion of his twelfth year." It would be interesting to know just how long it would require for the " industrial " school to get full possession of a boy who
had previously enjoyed a training exclusively " intellectual."

The quack doctor who, in his ignorance of his
patient's case, prescribes bread pills (under another
name) to be taken at intervals of two hours and seven
minutes, alternated with meal powders (also under
another name), has an eye to business. Such a knowledge of the wonderful mechanism of the human body,

and the chemical nature of the medicine put into it, so
perfectly estimating the beginning and end of effects,
is wonderful to behold, and inspires the implicit confidence of the hopeful patient. So the educator who so
claims ability to discern the "rise and fall" of faculty
as to be able to prescribe when the child should begin
to think or to use his hands, has been admired by those
who have more money to pay taxes than time to investigate the validity of the claim.

The committee dwell at some length on the evils of
"premature development," "arrested development,"
"preternatural acuteness," of street gamins, " Punch
and Judy faces," etc., as though these things had anything to do with the subject of their investigation. It
is one of the favorite methods of a bad cause to point
out existing social evils as casually related to the object of the aversion. That cause must, indeed, be a
desperate one which will attribute to the manual training school that class of influences which makes street
gamins and criminals of its students.

The report sounds a note of warning against impos-
ing on the child the "cares of mature life." It would
be a gratuitous assumption that would intimate that
manual exercise produces this result, or that it is unpleasant to the pupils. That the reverse of this is true
has been iterated and reiterated by pupils, patrons and
managers of manual training schools. The committee
themselves acknowledge this in another part of the report, when they say : " Boys may love the work of the
manual training school, and dislike history, grammar
and mathematics, and all book-learning, in fact." This
not only seems to contradict the " premature-cares-of
-life " plea, but furnishes another gratuitous assumption

that love for the manual training school means hatred
for other factors of education. These conflicting expressions seem to give the report more the appearance
of the special pleading of the mere advocate than of
the candid statement of the unbiased judge.

Whatever may be said of the advantages or disad-
vantages of the immunity of youth from responsibility,
it is curious that any one should believe that this immunity consists in preventing the pupil from exercising
his hands under mental guidance.

The juvenile phase of manual training seems to be
indorsed by the committee, if I correctly interpret the
meaning of the following somewhat ambiguous sen-
tence: "The work of the kindergarten, the schools for
waifs, and this line of effort, will stop the growth of that
hopeless class of society that has become arrested below the moral stage of development." This is a well-
deserved compliment to the kindergarten, but it is
expecting too much of it. Does the committee mean
that this "hopeless class that has become arrested below the moral stage of development" work their
children between the ages of two and eight years? and
that the kindergarten saves these children from this
"premature assumption of the cares of life?" If so, it
may be asked: "Does the kindergarten reach the class
of children referred to? What will become of them
after they leave the kindergarten? Are these good
influences, exerted during this brief period of infancy,
sufficient to "stop the growth" of that immoral branch
of society from which they sprung?

This acknowledges the potency of the manual element in education to a degree which would hardly be
ventured by the most ardent advocate of manual
raining.

The committee do not appear to regard the Kindergarten in the light of a manual training school. But wherein lies the difference between the Kindergarten and other methods of teaching children if not in the manual element? Why not anathematize those innovations of Frœbel as "trade schools?" The little ones build houses, construct bridges, erect forts, weave patterns, and make many other things suggestive of the "drudgery of life!" Let it be here noticed that any system of education which educates the pupil to look at labor as "drudgery" is a false and pernicious education, and the language of the report we are considering seems to indicate that this kind of education not only still exists but is advocated by the highest authority — the National Committee on Pedagogics. Is it not about time that we examine our ideals?

The report lays much stress on the "scientific view" that infancy and childhood should be protected from dwarfing influences. In this, they have clearly mistaken a scientific principle for an instance that is supposed to come under it. The truth of the principle will be admitted by all, but the use of it in supposing that manual training violates it and the schools as heretofore existing exemplify it, is an assumption which the facts do not justify.

A parallel to this is seen in the case of two boys who are eating fruit — one a peach, the other a banana. They dispute as to which kind is more healthful, when one of them vanquishes his adversary by quoting from his physiology lesson that, "that fruit is most healthful which best promotes digestion."

To the same effect the committee continue: "For there is a conviction deep seated in the minds of the people that all children ought to be educated together.in the humane studies that lie at the basis of liberal culture." But what are the "humane studies?" If it be the three R.'s, will the manual element neutralize any of the kindness which these indispensable studies may be supposed to have inculcated? If it be grammar, would the pupil become less sympathetic if allowed to alternate the use of the saw with his syntax? If it be history, would his hour in the shop rob him of the benevolence he had just inculcated from his study of human warfare and bloodshed? If it be rhetoric, would he lose the compassion which he had imbued while studying the laws of emotional expression if called upon during the next hour at the forge to tie up the burnt finger of a fellow student? If it be Greek, would he lose any of the mildness, tenderness, or mercy which the reading of the fables of the Odyssey had contributed to his character by forgetting for an hour at the bench that men were once changed into swine by royal fiat?

The committee would have the years of childhood and of youth free from anything like labor, that this period may be devoted to "spiritual growth," and the training of the will and intellect. That as they will not have time for these things when they are grown up they should lay in a stock while young sufficient to last them through life? If there is a kind of spirtuality to which the committee refer that grows without the exercise of the cardinal virtues which find their expression in the daily experiences of the daily industries and cares of life, then I will not pretend to discuss it. If they mean a species of will which grows in an atmosphere when the will is not exercised in self-denial, in performing unpleasant duties, and in overcoming difficulties, then I acknowledge my inability to speak of it. If there is a principle of growth which depends on influences of a nature different from those which the organism will be required to endure in maturity, then something new must have been recently discovered. Such a principle would have the oak grow in a warm shady spot and sheltered from the wind that it may better withstand the fierce storms to which the tree will be subjected in maturity.

This is not offered as an argument for increasing the cares and anxieties of childhood. I quite agree with the sentiment of the committee that this should as far as possible be avoided. But it is consideration of the stuff which spirituality and will-power are made of that induces me to call in question the quality of the ready-made article which the report prescribes.

Again : " The common school shall teach the pupil to conquer fortune by industry and good habits and the application of the tools of thought." If rightly interpreted this expresses a sound doctrine. If by tools of thought is meant the ability rationally to think in relations limited by the conditions of being, then no objection can be raised to this view of the province of the common school. Such a view makes the manual training school indispensable. But if by tools of thought is meant the mediæval tumor of abstract phrases which enables the possessor to cant about the unconditioned, then the tax-payer has a right to demur. Much that reaches the conventional standard of education is a mere flourish of the "tools of thought" without the thought. The workman is not known by his tools, but by his chips and the article produced.

"The trade or vocation in life is but a small part of

the total functions of any one's life" say the committee. Quite true, but it must not be forgotten that the trade or vocation is an *essential* part. It is idle to talk about the luxuries till the means for the essentials have been provided for. The manual element in education makes the luxuries possible by making the essentials sure. But the misguided pupil who has been taught to regard the essentials as "drudgery" will stand a poor chance of getting the luxuries. It seems strange that leading educators should feel called upon to treat with contempt the very conditions of existence. The entire report is a reflection of that false and pernicious type of education which despises labor and fills the land with "scholarly" upstarts who are incapable of earning an honest living.

The report dwells at some length discussing the dangers from the "illiterate manual labor." Is it possible that this committee believe that applies to any manual training school in existence? If so, then their ignorance of the facts makes the report valueless. It seems strange that an association representing the nation should appoint a committee to report on a question to which they had given no thought. The appointment by the officers of a county fair, of a dry goods merchant to award premiums for the best threshing machines, would be regarded bad management; and this would rarely happen unless the appointing power owned one of the machines.

The committee argue the uselessness of manual training from the advance made in machinery, which "does the drudgery of the work and leaves to the laborer only the task of supervision. The more complete the machine becomes the more operations it includes in its processes, the more intellect is required to manage it." But it may be asked at this point, Who completes the machine? Who invents it? Do inventions emanate from the so-called intellectual workers who have learned the laws of nature and the properties of matter from books? Who does not know that inventors are almost invariably either manual laborers or practical scientists whose manual or experimental efforts lead to discovery and invention? The common error with educators is in mistaking encyclopedic information about science for science itself. There is a difference between historical information *about* science and working *in* science. Is it to be supposed that a man educated in books alone is fit to supervise either the construction or the running of machinery? If there is doubt on this point let a college graduate of the conventional type apply for a position to "superintend machinery." The answer and the expression on the face of the man applied to might be suggestive. If the invention of machinery were dependent on that kind of "intellectual training" prescribed by the committee, some time would elapse before it would "emancipate the laborer."

Perhaps the most unsatisfactory and untrustworthy part of this report is where reference is made to the comparative value of "natural science in its general phases" with its "special applications to the theory of special machines." It is claimed that the former is "more lasting," that the latter "is but for a day." This is true of and applies only to the mere servile mechanical laborer, who without mental training works under the eye of another. It is not true of the student who builds the machine *for mental and manual culture.*

In building a single engine he will be brought face to

face with almost all the principles learned from his books. He has the opportunity, of correcting false notions which he is sure to get from book study alone. He here, and here only, can learn the true meaning of many of the technicalities of the text. The whole argument urged against the construction of machinery as an educative factor would have equal force against the laboratory method of studying physics and chemistry, and would run as follows: "Why soil the hands and consume time in experimenting when the theory of these operations involves all realizations of it?" The performance of the experiment admits of one of an indefinite number of "styles" of performance, uses one kind of reagent or apparatus "out of many, and encounters peculiar difficulties of one kind and another occasioned by temporary conditions that have nothing to do with the *nature* of the 'experiment' or with its performance elsewhere." For the student "thus obscures his general view of the principle of the 'experiment' by covering it up with a great collection of details *that do not essentially concern it.*" (Italics are mine.) Why not learn these things from the book and be done with it?

I am aware that this sort of argument when applied to laboratory work would be accepted by many still ranking themselves as educators, but it is hardly fair to suppose that this committee belong to that type. I shall assume therefore that they believe in experimental work in chemistry. They are philosophers —psychologists, and I would therefore like to hear from them on the following points : —

1. What is the physical advantage of performing a

chemical experiment over reading about the same from a book?

2. Will not the same advantage be realized in building a steam engine over the mere reading about it?

3. What is implied in a concept?

4. On what does the correctness or reliability of this concept depend?

5. What is the mental discipline and what is the student getting when he is trying to overcome "peculiar difficulties" in performing an experiment or in getting an engine to work?

6. What kind of exercise is he getting while struggling with "temporary conditions" which the theory does not provide for? or is it exercise at all?

7. What will be the relative value of the knowledge gained by this exercise after he has secured his position to "superintend machinery?"

Again: "The training of the muscles for a special operation unfits it more or less for the other special operations. * * * It fixes in his bodily organization certain limitations which unfit him for other occupations."

This implies that the exercises of the manual training school are pursued to the extent of fixing habit in special movements. It also implies that these habits when formed are pursued till the muscles of the student become set and rigid, which would further imply that the manual training school has a course extending over a period of fifteen to twenty-five years. Need it be said that no one of these implications is true? The united testimony of manual training school teachers and directors as well as that of common sense tell us that no fixed habits in any special movement can be formed during the brief period of school life, especially when these exercises are taken along with the other part of the curriculum.

The limitations of a trade could not fasten upon a school-boy. It is doubtful if even an artisan feels them till he has passed the meridian of life. It is quite true that "every trade has its special knack or skill," but no special training is aimed at in the manual training school. It is also true that the hammer and saw are among the tools used in the manual training school and are not used in a cotton factory. It is also true that geometry and trigonometry are tools (intellectual) used in all schools, but are not used in the practice of medicine. If the limitations of the use of the hammer and saw disqualify the factory hand, then why will not the limitations of geometry disqualify the physician? There is a mental dexterity and a manual dexterity, and both alike depend upon exercise for their development. To suppose that the exercises of a manual training school, be it what it may, disqualifies for any trade would find a parallel in the supposition that the common school "intellectual" branches which as taught are solely the tools of a teacher—disqualify for all other professions.

It will not do to say that "the course of study in manual training in so far as it concerns the education of the hand is limited to a narrow circle of trades in the wood and metal industries," for it is not true. The hand which moves under the guidance of the will is educated, and the process of education does not cease till that movement becomes automatic.

The only admission of the educative value of manual training which the committee make is the following:—

All laborers who employ machines or tools of any

description would be benefited to a greater or less degree by a course of manual training, and there is something educative in it for all who are to use machines. This is the most that can be urged by the advocates of the manual training school in behalf of its educative value.

This is an important admission and is alone sufficient to justify the existence of a manual training department in every high school in the country.   For the world's producers are tool users.   Man has even been called the tool-using animal.   He naturally takes to tools unless thwarted by a false and one-sided education.   But important as is the admission it is not sufficient.   The committee would have us believe that manual training is of no use to the lawyer, the physician, or the clergyman.   There is good reason to believe that this is a false assumption ; the exposition of the error is difficult and will appear of little force to those who are disposed to ignore the identity of mind and neural function.   Of course it is not denied that the nature of the mind is a profound mystery.   But the very best thought on the subject, of those who have looked most deeply into the matter both from the physiological and psychological side, agree that if the mind is not a function of the supreme neural centers of the cerebrum, it is so intimately connected therewith that any modification of the one is known always to be accompanied by corresponding modifications of the other.   Many of the impressions made through the senses are unconscious and produce modifications of mind.   We know that most distinguished men have, some time during their life, engaged in manual labor.   I do not believe that thoroughly healthy thought is possible without it.   The

reflex action between brain and hand is a necessary
condition of solid thinking. The mere metaphysician
is squabbling with words which have no definite meaning. He is a giant tugging away at his boot straps —
wrestling with first causes — "thinking" of the un-
thinkable.

The idea of a manual element in intellectuality is not
new. Anaxagoras, the master of Socrates, attributed
man's superiority over the lower animals to the fact of
his having hands. Maudsley says : " The muscles are
not alone the machinery by which the mind acts upon
the world, but their acts are essential elements in our
mental operations. The superiority of the human over
the animal mind seems to be essentially connected
with the greater variety of muscular action of which
man is capable. Were he deprived of the infinitely
váried movements of hands, tongue, larynx, lips, and
face in which he is so far ahead of the animals, it is probable that he would be no better than an idiot, notwith-
standing he might have a normal development of
brain." [Mind and Body, p. 32.]

Again he says: " We see that the supreme centers
are educated as other centers are, and the better they
are educated the better do they perform their functions
of thinking and willing. The development of mind is a
gradual process of organization in them. Ideas as they
are successively acquired through the gateways of
the senses are blended and combined and grouped in a
complexity that defies analysis; the organic combination
being the physiological conditions of our highest mental operations — reflection, reasoning, and judgment."

Thus a boy who works with his hands, learning the
properties of matter through sensation — the only true

source — enjoying that reflex action between hand and brain which constitutes the basis of sound thinking, is getting the impressions which are the physical conditions of ideas.   He is learning the elements of his true relations to the things of the world of which he is a part.

The mistake made by these people who do not recognize the educative value of manual training is in supposing that the manual experience of infancy and childhood is sufficient to last them through life.   They work over their meager sense experience into anomalous and monstrous products which they give names to, and then dispute over the names.   It is not enough to "educate" one side of a boy in this way and then label him Dr., D. D., or LL.D.   For knowing nothing of the character of the life work of those upon whom he depends for his support and whom from his education he regards beneath him, he is not in sympathy with the "lower classes."   This lessens his usefulness to them even if his education were of such a character as to benefit them.

Again I quote from the report: "The moral education in manual training, in the way of perseverance, patience, and plodding industry is a far greater factor than the intellectual factor."   Three paragraphs further on it reads: "Your committee would here call attention to other arguments often used which are weak and misleading, such for example, as the statement that manual training cultivates the powers of attention, perseverance, and industry. * * * To be excellent in manual training would not prevent him (the boy) from being illiterate and a bad neighbor and a bad citizen — even a dynamiter."   I shall not attempt to reconcile these two quotations.

Again: "The advocates of manual training admit that it is useful as education only if not carried to the point of arriving at skill in production. This feature of course makes against the economical argument in behalf of such schools." A parallel argument would run as follows: The advocates of the study of mathematics admit that it is useful education only if not carried to the point of arriving at skill in projecting bridges or other special applications. This feature of course makes against the economical argument in behalf of mathematical study! Similar parallels might be drawn with almost any branch of study.

The report concludes with a plea for industrial drawing, "as a training for the hand and eye and the æsthetic sense." For a production embodying educational doctrine of *form* this seems to be a fitting climax: "The object of the study of drawing in our schools is not the acquirement of a 'new art of expression' * * * because it is not worth the pains to learn the art of drawing merely to make pictures of what is seen or what is fancied. *Rather is drawing the best means of acquiring familiarity with the conventional forms of beauty in ornament.*"

It is difficult to treat such a doctrine as this with that gravity which properly belongs to the subject. Conventional forms of beauty in ornament to immature children! Not worth the pains to learn the art of drawing merely to make pictures of what is seen or fancied! To offer an adequate refutation to such pedagogical conclusion is not within the scope of this article. But if there are those among my readers who are inclined to accept statements and "doctrines" on authority, let them read along with it the following from Herbert

Spencer's "Education:" "The spreading recognition of drawing as an element of education is one amongst many signs of the more rational views on mental culture now beginning to prevail. Once more it may be remarked that teachers are at length adopting the course which nature has for ages been pressing upon their notice. The spontaneous efforts made by children to represent the men, houses, trees, and animals around them—on a slate if they can get nothing better, or with lead pencil on paper, if they can beg them—are familiar to all. * * * And these instinctive attempts to represent interesting actualities should be all along encouraged, in the conviction that, as by a widening experience, smaller and more practicable objects become interesting, they too will be attempted; and that so a gradual approximation will be made towards imitations having some resemblance to the realities. No matter how grotesque the shapes produced; no matter how daubed and glaring the colors. The question is not whether the child is producing good drawings—the question is, whether it is developing its faculties. * * * From all that has been said, it may be readily inferred that we wholly disapprove of the practice of drawing from copies, and still more so of that formal discipline in making straight lines and curved lines and compound lines, with which it is the fashion of some teachers to begin. * * * The work is, in short, a grammar of form with exercises. And thus the system of commencing with a dry analysis of elements, which, in the teaching of language, has been exploded, is reinstituted in the teaching of drawing. The abstract is to be preliminary to the concrete. Scientific conceptions are to precede empirical experi-

6

ences. That this is an inversion of the normal order, we need scarcely repeat. . It has been well said, concerning the custom of prefacing the art of speaking any tongue by a drilling in the parts of speech and their functions, that it is about as reasonable as prefacing the art of walking by a course of lessons on the bones, muscles, and nerves of the legs; and much the same thing may be said of the proposal to preface the art of representing objects by a nomenclature and definitions of the lines which they yield on analysis. These technicalities are alike repulsive and needless. They render the study distasteful at the very outset, and all with the view of teaching that which, in the course of practice, will be learnt unconsciously."

If the report of the National committee on pedagogics is a polemic, it evidently has the worst side of the question. If it is anything else, then either the committee are in possession of an insufficient number of facts, or I have failed to grasp their meaning.

Coming from so profound a thinker as Prof. Harris I can account for this report only by the supposition that under the pressure of other work he did not give it his best thought and attention.

APPENDIX.

REPORT OF THE COMMITTEE ON PEDAGOGICS, NATIONAL COUNCIL, JULY, 1889.

THE EDUCATIONAL VALUE OF MANUAL TRAINING.

The subject of the Educational Value of Manual Training has come to be of prime importance by reason of the strong claims set up for it by its advocates, and secondly, by reason of the fact that as a cause it serves to unite not only the critics of the educational system already existing, but also its uncompromising enemies ; thirdly, because the claims set forth in its behalf are based, not on economic reasons, but on educational reasons, an assumption being actually made that the effect of manual training on the pupil is educational in the same sense as the branches of science and literature heretofore taught, or at least if different from them, of equal or of superior value to them. This assumption unsettles the entire question of course of study, in so far as it rests on the doctrine of a specific educational value for each of the branches of the course of study, and in so far as it is supposed that the present list of branches provides for an all-sided intellectual training.

Your committee accordingly have proposed to themselves in this report to discuss the various phases of this assumption, and to inquire in what precisely consists the educational value of the branches taught in the manual training school, and wherein they are supplementary of the work already done, and wherein they cover the same ground. They have proposed to treat incidentally also the economic questions involved, inasmuch as the popularity of the movement

(85)

has its foundation in the conviction that if the schools teach manual training, all pupils will be fitted for useful industries before the age of leaving school for business.

1. Your committee in the outset admit the reasonableness of substituting a system of manual training in special schools, in so far as it can be done, for the old system of apprenticeship. That said apprenticeship has been and is wasteful of the time and talents of the pupils, is conceded; that a school devoted to the business of educating the youth in the essentials of his trade or vocation, is superior to the old system that employed the apprentice in all the drudgery of the establishment, and postponed his initiation in the essential matters of his trade. But your committee insist that such manual training ought not to be begun before the completion of the twelfth year of the pupil, nor before he has had such school instruction in the intellectual branches of school-work, namely, in reading, writing, arithmetic, geography, grammar and history, as is usually required by those statute laws enforced in enlightened States to prevent the too early employment of minors in the industries, and the neglect of their school education. Your committee understand that any amount of manual training conducted in a school is no equivalent for the school education in letters and science, and ought not to be substituted for it. They hold the opinion, moreover, that neither apprenticeship nor the industrial school should be allowed to take possession of the youth until the completion of his twelfth year at least; the fifteenth year is still better, because physical maturity is necessary for the formation of the best muscular movements to produce skill. At too early an age the pupil with his small hands and fingers, his short and undeveloped arms, is obliged to acquire bad habits of holding the implements of labor, just as a child that commences holding a pen too early will not hold it so as to secure freedom of movement. Moreover, the serious occupations of life cannot be imposed on children without dwarfing their human nature, physically, intellectually and

morally, and producing arrested development. Not only the games of youth, but the youth's freedom from the cares of mature life, should be insured to him if the best preparation is to be made for manhood. It is sad to know that very many children are dwarfed by family necessity, which compels them to bear the weights and cares of mature years. The street gamin in the city is preternaturally acute, but is not in process of growth towards ideal manhood. Later on he will be found suffering from premature old age, in every respect a wasted human life burnt out before it could develop its moral and intellectual ideals. He will have a " Punch and Judy " face such as Dickens ascribes to the stunted products of London street education. Students of anthropology tell us that man surpasses the animals so much in his mature life because he has a so much longer period of helpless infancy. He passes through a hundred grades of ascent above the brute, using all his forces in learning to walk on his hind legs, to use articulate speech 'for intercommunication, to dress himself in clothes, and to put on that far subtler clothing of customs and usages which hold back and conceal his animal propensities and substitute courtesy towards others for selfish natural impulse. Were it not for this diversion of the forces of childhood, man might develop like the animals the ability to walk immediately after birth, and use his bundle of intellectual instincts at once without the necessity of a long process of education. On these grounds your committee deprecate the necessities which abridge the period of childhood, and consider this one of the first reforms that social science is demanding. namely, the protection of children from the premature assumption of the cares of life. The work of the kindergarten, the schools for waifs, and this line of effort, will stop the growth of that hopeless class of society that has become arrested below the moral stage of development.

The ever present argument of the economical view of education calls attention to the fact that the great majority of children are destined to earn their living by manual labor. Hence, it is argued, the school ought to prepare them for their future work. The scientific view that lays so much stress on the protraction of the period of human infancy, is opposed to this demand for filling the child's mind with premature care for his future drudgery. In fact, this scientific doctrine has already been anticipated by the humane Christian sentiment which has founded public schools; for there is a conviction deep seated in the minds of the people that all children ought to be educated together in the humane studies that lie at the basis of liberal culture. Just for the very reason that the majority have before them a life of drudgery, the period of childhood, in which the child has not yet become of much pecuniary value for industry, shall be carefully devoted to spiritual growth, to training the intellect and will, and to building the basis for a larger humanity. Such a provision commends itself as an attempt to compensate in a degree for the inequalities of fortune and birth. Society shall see to it that the child who cannot choose the family in which he shall be born, shall have given him the best possible heritage that fortune could bring him, namely, an education that awakens him to the consciousness of the higher self that exists dormant in him. The common school shall teach him how to conquer fortune by industry and good habits, and the application of the tools of thought.

The economic, utilitarian opposition to the spiritual education in our schools comes before us to recommend that we forecast the horoscope of the child, and in view of his future possible life of drudgery make sure of his inability to ascend above manual toil by cutting off his purely intellectual training, and making his childhood a special preparation for industry.

Your committee would at this point call attention to the fatal omission on the part of the economist to see what is implied in his statement, that the schools should fit the child for his future duties in life. For when we inquire, we discover at once that the trade or vocation in life is but a small part of the total functions of any one's life. It is what goes with the trade or vocation that makes even it a success or failure. What does one need to know besides his trade? To this question your committee enumerate the following: —

1. Under the head of behavior toward others, his success will depend on the treatment of his fellow-workman and his employers; on his treatment of his neighbors, and of his family and children. Moreover, his behavior as a citizen concerns vitally all who live with him under the same government; for he conditions to the extent of his single vote, and the proletariat class as a whole may form a majority and determine altogether what sort of government shall be placed over all, rich and poor, Christian or heathen, humane or selfish. The " dude " citizen, who inherits large wealth and believes that the laboring classes should not be educated beyond the station they are to occupy in life, will find that the manual laborers are also voters, and that they decide whether there shall be rights of private property or protection of life and limb for him as well as for others.

The illiterate manual laborer, no matter how skillfully educated for his trade in wood and metal operations, cannot read and write. He cannot read the newspaper and take interest in the doings of town, State and nation or world at large, except as he hears of it in the turbid stream of personal gossip from fellow-workmen. He is essentially shut in, and his thoughts move around in a narrow circle like the horse that turns the wheel of the mill. Nothing can prevent his being the victim of wild schemes of agitation that attack radically all the institutions of civilization. To the observer of the newer and newest phases of modern history, nothing is so clear as the fact that the first necessity of civilization is a system of universal education, not in industry, but in the ideas and thoughts that make up the conventional view of the world — such ideas and opinions as one learns in studying geography and history, and especially literature.

2. Your committee would now call your attention, in the second place, to the educative phases of manual training. They admit that manual training is an educative influence; for all that man does or experiences is educative to him, and affects both his will and intellect. The education of the will takes place by fixing or unfixing habits of doing; the education of the intellect takes place through the ascent from one thought or idea to another; from a narrow point of view to a broader and more comprehensive one; from a vague and general grasp of a subject to an insight that explains all the details, and sees the relations of all parts to the whole.

In so far as manual-training schools teach the scientific principles that underlie the practical points of their work, they add intellectual education to physical education. Instruction in the natural sciences gives knowledge of nature, both as to its modes of existence and as to the forces that form and transform those modes of existence. Natural science, it will be readily admitted, is directly tributary to the emancipation of the laborer, because it leads more and more to the invention of machinery. Machinery does the drudgery of the work, and leaves to the laborer only the task of supervision; it assumes the physical labor, and gives him the intellectual labor of directing and managing it. The more complete the machine becomes, the more operations it includes in its process, the more intellect is required to manage it and the greater becomes its productiveness.

Compare the study of natural science in its general phases with its special applications of the theory of special machines, and it is seen that the study of the more general is more highly educative; and your committee would call special attention to the principle on which this conclusion is based. That is more highly educative which lasts longest and has widest scope in its enlightening effects. The explanation of the special machine (the steam engine, for example) is an intellectual acquisition for to-day; and it gives

one also a ready insight into all other examples to be met
with in future experience. But the study of the theories of
heat and of the dynamics of 'elastic fluids gives insight not
only into the steam engine, but also into a thousand other
applications (spouting geysers, oil wells, heating and ventil-
ating houses, meteorology, for example) within one's experience, and numberless thousands of examples possible in
future experience. Hence the study of pure science is more
educative intellectually than the study of special applications
of it.

Again, the study of applications of science is more educative than the labor of making the machine. The theory of
its operation involves all realizations of it, and is not exhaust-
ed until all real and possible varieties of construction have
been explained by it. But the construction of a machine
adopts one of an indefinite number of styles of construction,
uses one kind of material out of many for each of the parts,
and encounters peculiar difficulties of one kind and another
occasioned by temporary conditions that have nothing to do
with the nature of the machine or with its construction elsewhere. The laborer thus obscures his general view of the
principle of the machine by covering it up with a great collection of details that do not essentially concern it. He is
much more impressed with accidental matters of no account
in the theory of the working of the machine, than he is with
the principles of its action. In a second experiment at constructing a machine, old difficulties disappear and new ones
arise. The intellectual education is of narrow scope and
limited in time.

The intellectual factor of manual labor is never very large
even in the first construction of a new type of product.
The moral education in manual training in the way of perseverance, patience, and plodding industry, is a far greater
educational factor than the intellectual factor.

The education of the muscles of the hand and arm, the
training of the eye in accuracy, go for something in the

way of education, especially if these, too, are of a general
character, and productive of skill in many arts. But it happens in most cases that the training of the muscles for a
special operation unfits it more or less for the other special
operations. Every trade has its special knack or skill, and
not only requires special education to fit the laborer to pursue it, but it reacts on him, and fixes in his bodily organism
certain limitations which for greater or less extent unfit him
for other occupations. The work of blacksmithing, for instance, would unfit one for engraving; the work in planing
and sawing would diminish the skill of the wood-carver.
Work in the trades that deal with wood and metals (and these
include the entire curriculum of the manual-training school)
would be disadvantageous to the delicate touch required by
the laborer on textile manufactures; and this class of laborers is nearly as large as the combined classes of wood
and metal workers.

Your committee find that the course of study in manual
training, in so far as it concerns the education of the hand,
is limited to a narrow circle of trades in the wood and metal
industries, and that so far as it is auxiliary to trades and occupations directly, it covers the work of only one in twelve
of the laborers actually employed in the United States.

Indirectly, as dealing especially with the construction of
machinery, it has a much wider application, and your committee believe that all laborers who employ machines or tools
of any description would be benefited to a greater or less
degree by a course of manual training, and that there is
something educative in it for all who are to use machines.
This is the most important argument that can be urged by
the advocates of the manual-training school in behalf of its
educative value.

Your committee would here call attention to other arguments often used which are weak and misleading; such, for
example, as the statement that manual training cultivates the
powers of attention, perseverance, and industry. These are

formal powers, and not substantial; that is to say, they derive their value from what they are applied to, and they may be mischievous as well as beneficial. The power of attention may be cultivated by the game of chess, or the game of whist, or of draw poker, or to the picking of pockets; but it is only attention to those subjects and not attention in general that is cultivated. The whist-player who has developed careful circumspection, keen attention, the calculation of probabilities in the matter of cards, is quite likely not to manifest them in regard to higher matters of observation of nature or the study of man. All games of boys — for instance marbles, quoits, base ball, jacks-straws — are educative. especially in such matters as are named as results of manual training. namely : (a) the development of the physical powers ; (b) the acquisition of dexterity of hand and accuracy of eye ; (c) in perseverance ; (d) in attention. These moreover carry with them some general training, and give the boy a similar ability in a field of related subjects. But it would not be fair to expect that these qualities of mind would show themselves in the boy's work in mathematics or history, for his interest in these games might make him dull and inattentive to all school studies. Boys may love the work of the manual-training school and dislike history, grammar. and mathematics, and all book-learning, in fact; but to be excellent in manual training would not prevent him from being illiterate and a bad neighbor and a bad citizen — even a dynamiter.

Your committee would further call attention to the fact that what is educative at one time may be entirely without such an effect at another — or, indeed, it may be deadening to the mind. Thus the advocates of manual training admit that it is useful as education only if not carried to the point of arriving at skill in production. This feature, of course, makes against the economical argument in behalf of such schools. According to the economic view, skill in production is the primary object aimed at by introducing the training of the hand into schools. But M. Sluys, the Belgian normal school director who reports on the Swedish system, says that when the child is compelled to manufacture large numbers of a given object in order to acquire skill in the work, the educative value of the work diminishes. "From the third or fourth sample his interest wanes; mechanical repetition invariably excites disgust for any work."

Your committee would call attention here to the fact that if an educative opportunity is gained by not requiring mechanical repetition to the point of acquiring skill, there is also an educative opportunity lost; for the patience and perseverance that pursues its work to the end, and bravely keeps down any tendencies to disgust at the lack of novelty, is a moral education indispensable to success in any manual calling. No teaching in the studies of the schools as they are would be esteemed of a high order if it did not train its pupils to attack difficult studies like arithmetic and grammar and courageously overcome them. Mere natural disinclination and impatience must be conquered before the child can become a rational being.

Your committee would further suggest, that no justice as yet has been done by the advocates of manual training to the claims of industrial drawing as a training for the hand and eye and the æsthetic scene. If the pupil pursues this study by the analysis of the historical forms of ornament, and acquires familiarity with graceful outlines and a genuine taste for the creation of beautiful and tasteful forms, he has done more towards satisfying the economic problem of industry than he could do by much mechanical skill. The great problem in the industry of nations has come to be the æsthetic one — how to give attractive and tasteful forms to productions so as to gain and hold the markets of the world. The object of the study of drawing in our schools is not the acquirement of a "new art of expression," to use the stale definition put forward by some of the advocates of the self-styled "new education," because it is not worth the pains to learn the art of drawing merely to make pictures of what is seen or what is fancied. Rather is drawing the best means of acquiring familiarity with the conventional forms of beauty in ornament — forms that express the outlines of freedom and gracefulness and charm all peoples, even those who have not the skill to produce such forms. Some nations, like the French, for example, have educated their working classes for many generations in this matter of taste, and it has become a second nature. Other nations, the Anglo-Saxon among them, are not naturally gifted with a taste for the production of the beautiful, but rather with a tendency to look for the dynamic. the lines of force rather than of freedom. They are content to produce what is strong and durable and useful. But this has led them to the discovery that they must also be content with inferior places in international expositions, and with a virtual exclusion from the markets of the world. Only a high tariff can force any considerable consumption of useful articles of clumsy and unsightly shapes.

In view of these facts, your committee have deemed it desirable to mention industrial drawing and the true method of teaching it by the analysis and production of the standard ideals in ornament, as worthy of most careful consideration on the part of all, and especially on the part of all interested in manual-training instruction, either for its economical or its educative advantages.   Respectfully submitted.

GEORGE P. BROWN,   S. S. PARR,

J. II. HOOSE,   W. T. HARRIS,

Committee on Pedagogics.

www.ingramcontent.com/pod-product-compliance
Lightning Source LLC
Chambersburg PA
CBHW032247080426
42735CB00008B/1039